I0814143

Collins

SPACE TOUR

THE ULTIMATE JOURNEY ACROSS THE UNIVERSE

Written by Charlotte Isham and Dhara Patel

Published by Collins
An imprint of HarperCollins Publishers
1 Robroyston Gate, Glasgow G33 1JN

www.collins.co.uk

HarperCollins Publishers
Macken House, 39/40 Mayor Street Upper,
Dublin 1, Ireland D01 C9W8

First published 2025

Written by: Charlotte Isham & Dhara Patel
Cover design by: Rachael Horner

Publisher: Michelle l'Anson
Project leader: Beth Rogers
Designers: Kevin Robbins & James Hunter
Mission timeline illustrations: James Hunter
Editorial: Craig Balfour, Stella Caldwell, Julianna Dunn
Production: Ilaria Rovera

A catalogue record for this book is available from the British Library.

ISBN 978-0-00-875280-4

Printed by Replika Press, India

10 9 8 7 6 5 4 3 2 1

This book contains FSC™ certified paper and other controlled sources to ensure responsible forest management.

For more information visit: www.harpercollins.co.uk/green

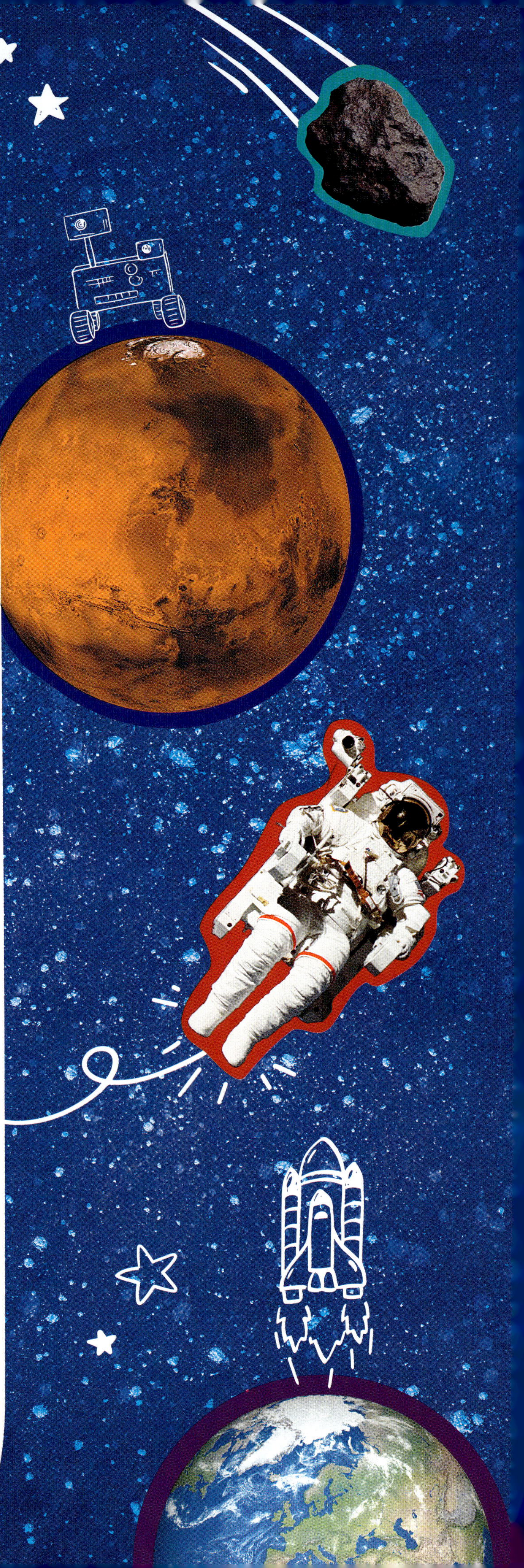

Contents

WHERE ARE WE IN THE UNIVERSE? · · · 4

THE SOLAR SYSTEM · · · 6

SPACE 101 · · · 8

ROCKY PLANETS · · · 10

GAS PLANETS · · · 28

MOONS · · · 46

SPACE ROCKS · · · 64

STARS · · · 82

GALAXIES · · · 104

INVISIBLE SPACE · · · 120

GLOSSARY · · · 140

INDEX · · · 142

Where are we in the Universe?

Have you ever wondered how big space is and where we are within it? In this book, you're going to take a tour through the Universe, exploring all the amazing and wonderful things inside it – starting by taking a look at our cosmic address, by zooming in from the wider Universe right into our Solar System. Let's go!

Measurements

1 AU (astronomical unit) = **150 million km**

1 LY (light-year) = **9.5 trillion km**

The Universe

The Universe is all of space and everything in it!

Zoom in!

The Milky Way

The Milky Way is one of around two trillion galaxies in our Universe.

Zoom in again!

The Milky Way is 100,000 LY across

Scale

1,000 = **1 thousand**

10,000 = **10 thousand**

100,000 = **100 thousand**

1,000,000 = **1 million**

1,000,000,000 = **1 billion**

1,000,000,000,000 = **1 trillion**

1,000,000,000,000,000,000,000,000 = **1 septillion**

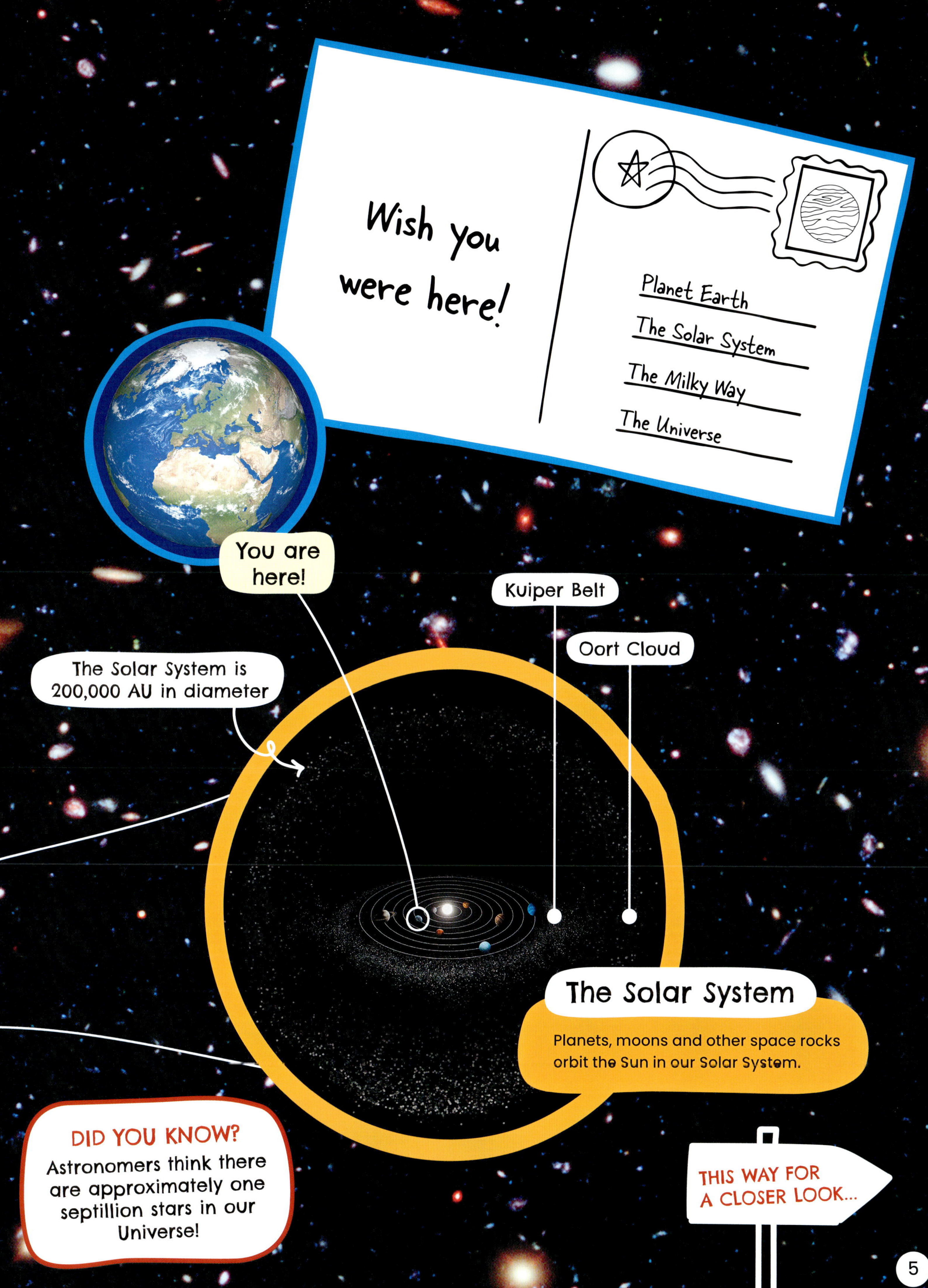

The Solar System

Planets, moons and other space rocks orbit the Sun in our Solar System.

DID YOU KNOW?

Astronomers think there are approximately one septillion stars in our Universe!

THIS WAY FOR A CLOSER LOOK...

The Solar System

Arriving in our Solar System, you'll see that there are inner planets and outer planets all travelling around our Sun. As you journey through the book, you'll take a closer look at these objects (and more!) to learn about the different types of missions that have explored them so far, and the fascinating discoveries that have been made!

Planets

There are eight main planets in our Solar System, moving around our Sun.

Sun

Our Sun is a star made of hot gasses. It is at the centre of our Solar System.

Venus

Saturn

Mars

Neptune

Asteroid Belt

Comets of the Kuiper Belt

DID YOU KNOW?

There are objects smaller than planets which also orbit the Sun, including dwarf planets, comets and asteroids.

Outer planets

The gas planets, also known as the outer planets, are the four planets farthest away from the Sun: Jupiter, Saturn, Uranus and Neptune. Their orbits lie outside of the asteroid belt.

Inner planets

The rocky planets, also known as the inner planets, are the four planets closest to the Sun: Mercury, Venus, Earth and Mars. Their orbits lie within the asteroid belt.

Jupiter

Uranus

Mercury

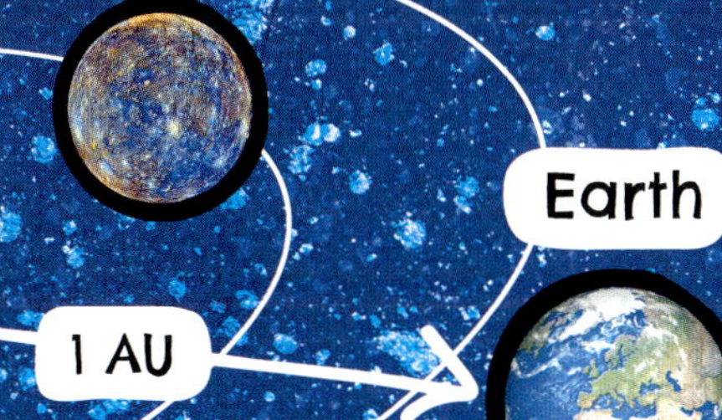

DID YOU KNOW?
There are many space agencies around the world doing research and exploring outer space, including NASA (United States), ESA (Europe), ROSCOSMOS (Russia), CNSA (China), JAXA (Japan) and ISRO (India).

Mission Keywords:

Flyby = flies past a planet or object in space

Orbiter = circles around a planet or object in space

Lander = lands in one spot on a planet or object in space

Rover = lands and moves around on a planet or object in space

Impactor = deliberately collides with a planet or object in space

Sample return = brings back samples from another planet or object in space

SOLAR SYSTEM

OORT CLOUD

KEEP GOING!

Space 101

Before you set off on your mission, there are a few things you should know to help you along the way. Don't worry, you can always come back to this page to remind yourself of any of these keywords. Once you've completed this checklist, you'll be ready to launch – 3, 2, 1... Blast off!

Earth's magnetic field

Mass

Mass is the amount of stuff an object is made of. This number stays constant.

Gravity

Everything made of matter (stuff) has gravity, which pulls on other stuff around it. The more stuff, the greater the force of gravity.

Forces

Magnetic field

A magnet can attract or repel other magnetic materials like iron or nickel. A magnetic field is the region around a magnetic object where this invisible force acts.

Weight

Weight changes depending on gravity. For example, you would have the same mass on Earth as on the Moon – but because the force of gravity is weaker on the Moon, you would weigh less.

Light

Types of light

The light spectrum is made up of a variety of light. This includes visual light, which we can see with our eyes, and other invisible types of light, such as infrared or ultraviolet.

Speed of light

Light is the fastest thing we know and travels in straight lines at a speed of 300,000 kilometres per second.

Ultraviolet

Visible

Infrared

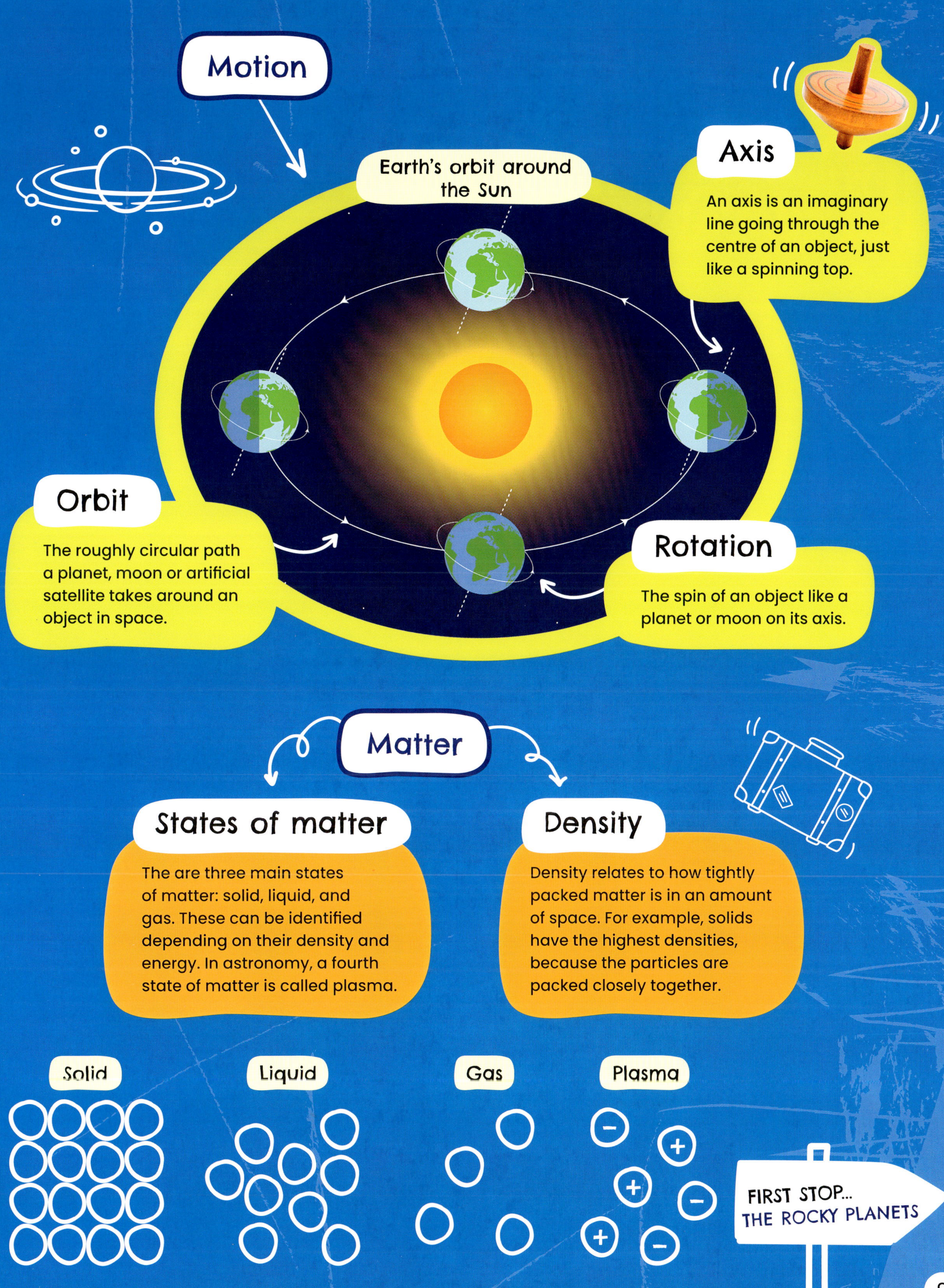
Motion
Earth's orbit around the Sun
Axis
An axis is an imaginary line going through the centre of an object, just like a spinning top.
Orbit
The roughly circular path a planet, moon or artificial satellite takes around an object in space.
Rotation
The spin of an object like a planet or moon on its axis.
Matter
States of matter
The are three main states of matter: solid, liquid, and gas. These can be identified depending on their density and energy. In astronomy, a fourth state of matter is called plasma.
Density
Density relates to how tightly packed matter is in an amount of space. For example, solids have the highest densities, because the particles are packed closely together.
Solid
Liquid
Gas
Plasma
FIRST STOP...
THE ROCKY PLANETS

Rocky Planets

First up, the four rocky planets in our Solar System! As they're the closest to the Sun, they're often called the inner planets. During this exploration of our star's closest neighbours, marvel at their amazing features and discover how humanity has learned so much about them!

Mercury

Mercury is a planet of extremes – it has huge temperature swings, it's peppered with craters and it has almost no atmosphere. Because of this, it's one of the least likely places for life in our Solar System. If we could live there, we'd have to get used to some strange things – days twice as long as a year, and a Sun that looks three times bigger in the sky than it does on Earth.

Quick Facts

Moons = **0**

Size = **4,880 km in diameter**

Average temperature = **167°C**

Length of rotation = **59 Earth days**

Length of year = **88 Earth days**

Average distance from the Sun = **58 million km or 0.4 AU**

Fastest planet

Mercury zips around the Sun at an astonishing speed of 47 kilometres per second. Because it's the closest planet to the Sun, the Sun's powerful gravity has a stronger pull on it – making Mercury's orbit quicker than any other planet in the Solar System.

Magritte, the 'Mickey Mouse' crater on Mercury

Countless craters

Like the Moon, Mercury is covered in craters – in photos, it can be hard to tell the two apart! One reason for the planet's pockmarked appearance is its lack of atmosphere, which gives little protection against impacts from space objects like asteroids. Another is that Mercury has no weather, such as wind or rain, to erode the craters away. Geologists call the largest craters – those more than 300 kilometres in diameter – 'basins'.

Eccentric planet

Mercury's orbit is the most eccentric, or oval-shaped, of any planet in our Solar System. Its distance from the Sun can vary wildly from 47 million to 70 million kilometres.

DID YOU KNOW?

Mercury is sometimes known as the 'oven and freezer' because it experiences extreme temperatures. Due to its lack of atmosphere, the temperature can rise to a sizzling 430°C during the day, while at night, it can plummet to around -180°C.

Fierce suntan

As the closest planet to the Sun, Mercury gets blasted by powerful solar energy – giving it an extreme 'suntan'. Dust and gas atoms are stripped away from the planet, because Mercury has almost no atmosphere to protect itself from the powerful solar particles that hit its surface. These cause it to produce X-rays and glowing auroras.

Thin shield

Mercury's small size means it doesn't have enough gravity to hold on to a thick atmosphere. And because it's so close to the Sun, powerful solar winds strip away most of the gas trying to stick around. But Mercury is just able to hold on to a super-thin layer called an exosphere – which separates the planet from the vacuum of space.

Iron core

Earth is the densest planet in our Solar System, but Mercury comes a close second! Its huge iron core makes up about 70 per cent of its mass and stretches across 85 per cent of its radius – making Mercury heavy for its small size. When the planets formed, those closer to the Sun swallowed up more iron than those further away.

1 TON

Seasonless

Unlike most other planets, Mercury and Venus don't have seasons. This is because the axis (the imaginary line) that these planets rotate around is tilted by less than 3 degrees, so they spin nearly completely upright.

Mercury missions (launch dates)

Mariner 10 (flyby)
3 Nov 1973

MESSENGER (orbiter)
2 Aug 2004

BepiColombo (orbiter)
20 Oct 2018

Venus

Although Venus is known as the Earth's twin due to its similar size and rocky nature, it is a deadly planet – one that would be almost impossible to survive on. Venus is the third brightest object in our sky but its thick, hazy atmosphere makes it difficult for spacecraft to peer down and see its surface. Beneath the clouds are flat, volcanic domes, towering mountains and hundreds of craters.

Quick Facts

Moons = **0**

Size = **12,104 km in diameter**

Average temperature = **475°C**

Length of rotation = **243 Earth days**

Length of year = **225 Earth days**

Average distance from the Sun = **108 million km or 0.72 AU**

Signs of life?

In 2020, astronomers thought they had found phosphine in Venus's atmosphere. This gas smells like mouldy fish or garlic. It's produced by small bacteria that live in areas where there is no oxygen, and it's also found in penguin poo! Could Venus harbour life after all?

Illustration of a volcano on Venus

Under pressure

On top of its intense heat and toxic gases, Venus also has very high pressure – almost 90 times higher than Earth's! This is like being 900 metres under water, which makes it very difficult for spacecraft to land on the planet. Future missions to Venus will probably use landers made of the tough metal titanium to survive the extreme conditions.

Venus missions (launch dates)

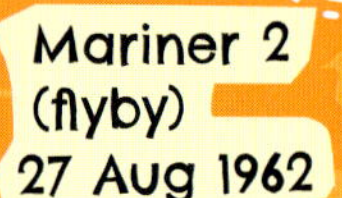

Mariner 2 (flyby) 27 Aug 1962

Pioneer Venus (orbiter) 20 May 1978

Sluggish Venus

A day (or complete rotation) on the planet is longer than a year! Venus is the slowest-spinning planet in our Solar System, taking more time to rotate once on its axis than to travel all the way around the Sun.

DID YOU KNOW?

Compared to the other planets, Venus spins backwards! It's thought that something may have crashed into the planet long ago, flipping the way it rotates. If you were standing on Venus, you'd see the Sun rise in the west and set in the east.

A watery past?

On Earth and Mars, there are signs that water carved out their landscapes, but this is not the case on Venus – and even its deep interior is believed to be much drier than Earth's. Scientists used to think that Venus was once warm and wet, but we now know it probably never had the right conditions for oceans to exist.

Poisonous atmosphere

Most of Venus's atmosphere is made up of carbon dioxide – in fact, it's nearly 97 per cent of it. This is one of the gases that contribute to the greenhouse effect on Earth. Along with clouds of poisonous sulfuric acid, this seems to make Venus a less suitable planet for life.

Venera 13
(flyby & lander)
30 Oct 1981

The Venera programme ran from 1965–1983

Megellan
(orbiter)
4 May 1989

Venus Express
(orbiter)
9 Nov 2005

Akatsuki
(orbiter)
20 May 2010

BepiColombo
(multiple flybys)
20 Oct 2018

Earth

Earth is the only known planet with life. It's home to millions of different animals and plants as well as many amazing environments. Humans have made incredible progress that has led to many benefits, but we also have a huge impact on Earth – more than any other living thing or natural force. That's why it's so important to take care of our home planet – there's no other place like it!

Quick Facts

Moons = **1**

Size = **12,760 km in diameter**

Average temperature = **15°C**

Length of rotation = **23.9 hours**

Length of year = **365.25 days**

Distance from the Sun = **150 million km or 1 AU**

Just right!

Our planet is situated at just the right distance from the Sun, in a special area called the Goldilocks zone (or the habitable zone). This means it's neither too hot nor too cold for liquid water to exist. In our Solar System, the Goldilocks zone stretches from just past Venus's orbit to Mars's orbit. This perfect spot means Earth is home to millions of different and amazing species!

Evolving Earth

Having formed 4.5 billion years ago, the Earth has changed dramatically in its lifetime. Beginning as a ball of molten rock it cooled to form a layered rocky planet. It's developed an atmosphere, become covered in oceans and seen the evolution of lots of life – the first of which likely appeared around 3.7 billion years ago.

Protective shield

The slow-moving molten iron in Earth's core creates the planet's magnetic field. This shield protects us from harmful radiation and charged particles given off by the Sun. Just like a bar magnet, Earth has a magnetic north and south pole, which is why we can use a compass to navigate.

Underwater waterfall in Mauritius

Water world

Liquid water is an important factor for life to exist on Earth. Over 70 per cent of the Earth's surface is covered in water, and the oceans hold nearly 97 per cent of the planet's water. The vast oceans also contain most of the world's volcanoes and huge mountain ranges, deep underwater.

Earth missions (launch dates)

V2
20 Feb 1947
Fruit flies become the first living organisms sent to space

DID YOU KNOW?

Earth has some extreme environments where we wouldn't expect life to exist. From scorching volcanoes and the freezing polar regions, to salty lakes and the dark depths of the oceans. But organisms called 'extremophiles' have adapted to live in these unusual places.

Plate tectonics

Earth's outer layer, the crust, is made up of massive 'plates' that fit together like a jigsaw puzzle – a bit like a cracked eggshell. These uneven slabs of solid rock are moved by the semi-liquid mantle layer below. This tectonic movement creates mountains, earthquakes, volcanic eruptions and ocean trenches.

What a mess!

Earth has thousands of artificial satellites orbiting around it, with the largest being the International Space Station. But there's even more space junk and debris floating around, created by rocket launches, broken satellites and collisions. There are more than 40,000 pieces bigger than 10 centimetres and over 130 million pieces smaller than 1 centimetre!

Sputnik 1
4 Oct 1957
First satellite

TIROS-1
1 Apr 1960
First weather satellite

Telestar 1
10 Jul 1962
First telecommunications and televised pictures

MIR
20 Feb 1986
First modular space station

ISS
20 Nov 1998
Longest-running space station

Mars

Mars is named after the Roman god of war. It's only about half the size of Earth, but it has some of the biggest features in our cosmic neighbourhood, making it an interesting and exciting place to explore. At first glance, the Red Planet might seem very different from Earth, but it's actually the most Earth-like planet in our Solar System!

Quick Facts

Moons = **2**

Size = **6,780 km in diameter**

Average temperature = **-65°C**

Length of rotation = **24.6 Earth hours**

Length of year = **687 Earth days**

Average distance from the Sun = **228 million km or 1.5 AU**

Potato moons

Spot the difference!

The two moons of Mars, Phobos and Deimos, are named after the Greek gods of fear and dread. This strange-shaped pair look more like giant space potatoes! Whilst Deimos zooms around Mars once every 30 hours, Phobos orbits closer to its planet than any other known moon – whipping around it three times a day!

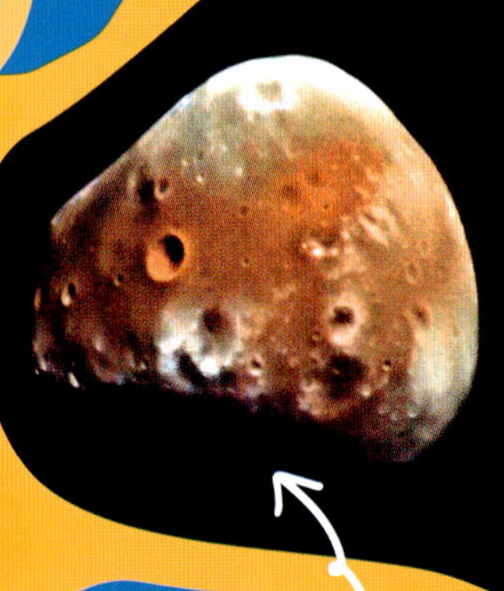

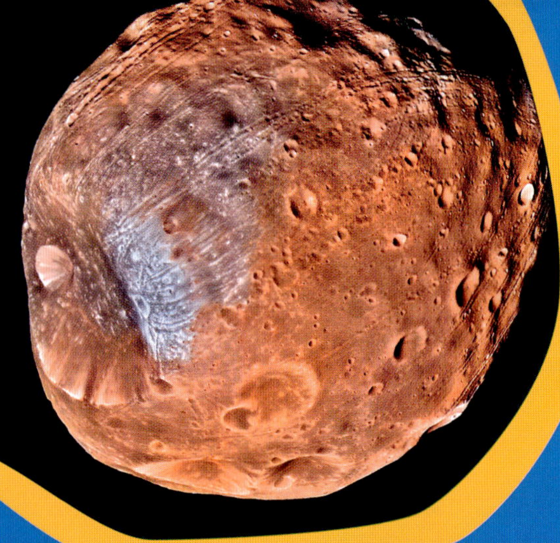

Deimos

Olympus Mons

Enormous volcano

Mars is home to the largest volcano in our Solar System – Olympus Mons. It's nearly three times the height of Mount Everest, but don't let that fool you – the base is about the size of France! Olympus Mons is a shield volcano. This means lava flows and spreads easily, creating a wide, gentle slope compared to the steeper volcanoes found on Earth.

Mars missions (launch dates)

Mariner 4 (flyby) 28 Nov 1964

Mars 2 (orbiter) 19 May 1971

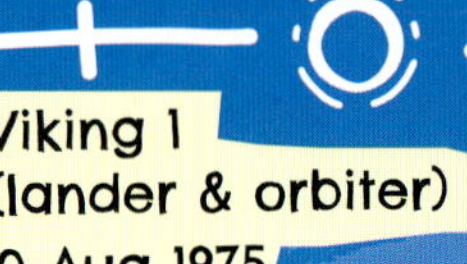

Viking 1 (lander & orbiter) 20 Aug 1975

Blue sunsets

The sky on Mars is the opposite to what we see on Earth – during the day it is a reddish colour and at sunset it looks blue. This is because Mars has much more fine dust in its atmosphere, which causes the light to be scattered differently.

Precious samples

Space missions have brought back rock and dust from the Moon and from asteroids - next on the list is samples from Mars! The precious specimens will need to be kept safe to avoid contamination and to prevent possible outbreaks if they contain anything harmful. The Double Walled Isolator system in Leicester, UK, is designed to do just that.

Olympus Mons

The Grandest of Canyons

Mars also boasts the largest canyon in our Solar System – Valles Marineris. It stands like a huge scar across the surface of the planet, and scientists believe it was formed as the planet cooled billions of years ago, or maybe by erosion or tectonic activity. It is truly impressive at around 4,000 kilometres long, 200 kilometres wide and 10 kilometres deep.

DID YOU KNOW?

The planet's red colour might make you think it's hot, but that's not the case. Mars gets its reddish hue from iron in its dust, rocks and soil, which has oxidised or rusted.

Mars Pathfinder (Sojourner – first rover operated on another planet) 4 Dec 1996

Spirit (rover) 10 Jun 2003

Opportunity (rover) 8 Jul 2003

Phoenix (lander with digging arm) 4 Aug 2007

Tianwen-1 (orbiter) 23 Jul 2020

Perseverance & Ingenuity (rover & helicopter) 30 Jul 2020

Fantastic features

The rocky planets are easy to recognise because of their unique appearances. But although they're quite different from each other, they still share some similarities – from their geological features to their surfaces and interiors.

Water relief!

Water exists in different amounts on different planets, but where it came from is still a mystery! Earth has plenty of water, while Mercury has ice hidden in deep craters at its poles. Mars shows signs of a watery past, and scientists think there's still water trapped deep below its surface. But Venus is dry and probably never had the right conditions for oceans to form.

Volcanoes

The four inner planets have experienced volcanic activity at some point in their history. Mars is home to the largest volcano in our Solar System, while Venus has the most volcanoes – more than 1,600 major ones! Astronomers believe that some of them may still be active today. On the other hand, Mercury is unlikely to have had much volcanic activity in billions of years.

Icy poles

When we think of polar ice, we usually imagine the frozen water in Earth's Arctic and Antarctic regions. But other rocky planets have polar ice too! On Mercury this can be found in the form of water ice, protected by the shadows of craters, whereas on Mars the frozen ice caps are formed not just of water but also of up to 85 per cent carbon dioxide in places.

Mars

Iron to the core

Deep inside every rocky planet is an iron core. Studying these cores helps scientists understand how planets formed and how our Solar System began. Whether a planet's core is solid or molten affects the formation and strength of its magnetic field.

Why are planets round?

Imagine holding a few marshmallows close together. The gaps between their odd shapes make something that isn't round. But more massive objects (at least a few hundred kilometres in size) have stronger gravity, which pulls everything towards the centre more tightly. This force pulls equally in all directions, causing massive objects like planets to become round.

Galle

Did you see that?

People often spot familiar shapes or patterns in unrelated objects – something that is known as 'pareidolia' (par-uh-DOH-lee-uh). On Venus, some volcanic features look like spiders, while the 'Face on Mars' is an eerie rock formation that appears to have eyes, a nose and a mouth. There's even a crater on Mars called Galle that looks like a smiley face!

Magnetic fields

All the rocky planets have magnetic fields, but they vary in strength and how they're formed. Mars once had a magnetic field, but it disappeared around 4 billion years ago as the planet cooled and the iron core 'shut down'. Without this protective shield, the Sun gradually stripped away Mars's atmosphere, leaving it exposed and vulnerable.

Impact craters

Craters are some of the most striking features on rocky planets. Mercury is covered with tens of thousands, making them easy to spot. Venus's thick atmosphere means the planet is much better protected, and many smaller objects burn up before reaching its surface. Earth falls somewhere in between – while smaller objects burn up in the atmosphere, our planet still has visible craters like the Arizona Meteor Crater. However, many craters have been hidden by weathering or are buried beneath layers of ice and rock.

Arizona Meteor Crater, USA

Astronomical wonders

From Earth, we get to witness all sorts of amazing astronomical events – some that guide us through the seasons and others that treat us to stunning sights in the sky. Understanding how the planets move and interact with the Sun helps us to predict these wonders – and enjoy them even more!

DID YOU KNOW?
Every planet that has a tilted axis will experience seasons and solstices.

Solstices

Solstices happen twice each orbit and are sometimes known as the longest or shortest days of the year. This happens when one of the poles of the Earth is most tilted towards the Sun with the other tilted away. When tilted towards the Sun we experience the longest hours of daylight and when angled away we have the shortest hours of daylight. In the Northern Hemisphere, the summer solstice happens around 20-21 June and the winter solstice around 21-22 December. This is the opposite in the Southern Hemisphere.

Season starters

The word 'equinox' comes from Greek, where 'equi' means equal and 'nox' means night. On Earth, there are two equinoxes a year – around 21–22 March and 21–22 September – when day and night are equal in length. Equinoxes also mark the start of spring or autumn, depending on whether you're in the Northern or Southern Hemisphere. All planets, except Mercury and Venus, are tilted on their axes, and experience seasons and equinoxes as a result.

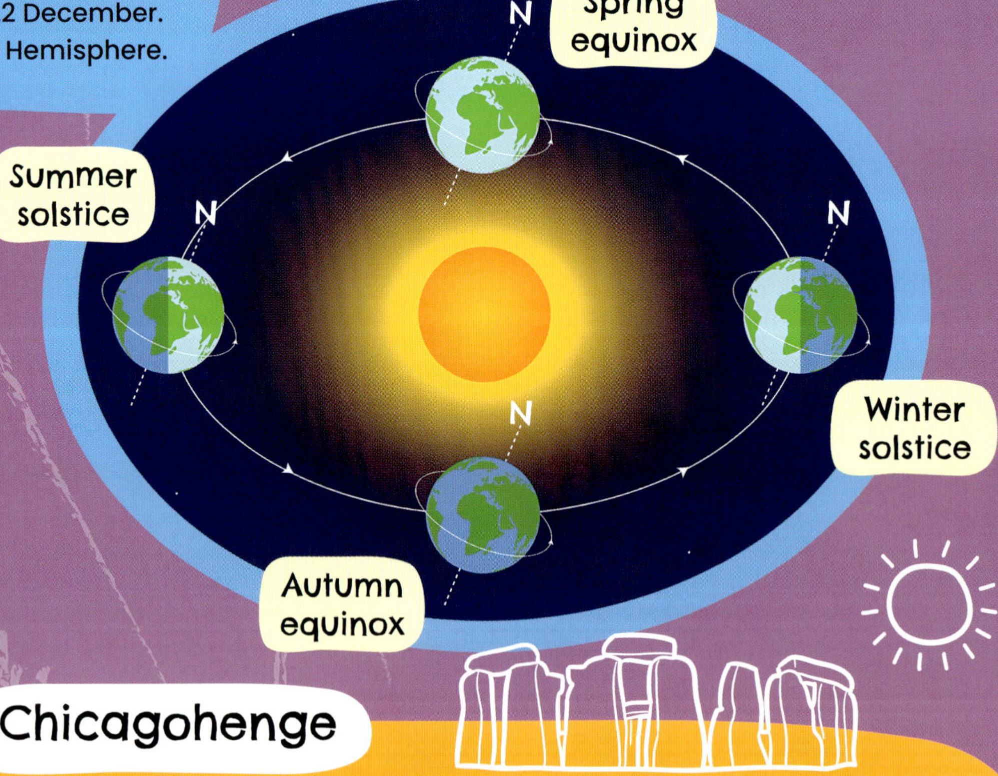

Chicagohenge, USA

Chicagohenge

Stonehenge – a famous prehistoric rock monument in Wiltshire, England – was built to line up with the rising and setting Sun on the solstices. In Chicago, USA, the skyscrapers are arranged in a grid pattern, and during the equinoxes, the Sun shines directly down the city's east-to-west running streets at sunrise and sunset. This amazing spectacle is called 'Chicagohenge'.

Brilliant Venus

Venus is the third brightest object in the sky, after the Sun and the Moon. Because of this, it's often called the 'Morning Star' or the 'Evening Star'. As Venus orbits the Sun, it's usually the first 'star' you see after the Sun sets – and the last one you see before the Sun rises.

Egg-shaped orbits

Planets don't all travel around the Sun in a perfectly circular orbit. For many planets these are more oval and stretched. This means at certain points in their orbit they can be much closer to Sun and we call this 'perihelion', and at other points they are further away from the Sun and we call this 'aphelion'. These differences can lead to changes in weather and affect the seasons on a planet.

Tick tock, change the clocks!

Many countries around the world change their clocks by an hour during the summer, to make better use of the daylight hours. Only three European countries (Iceland, Belarus and Russia) keep their clocks constant all year. Daylight Saving Time was first proposed by the inventor Benjamin Franklin as a way to save on candles!

Nature's light show

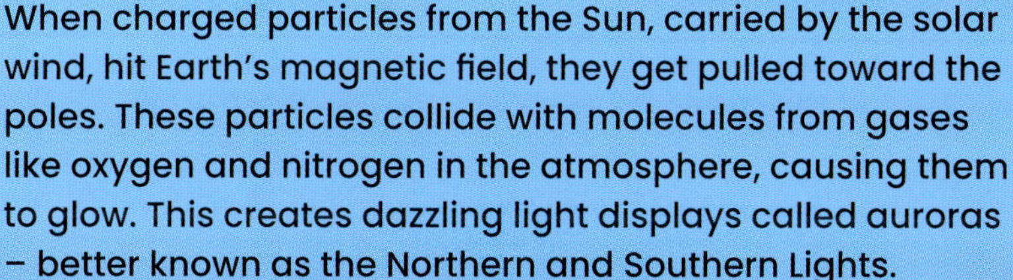

When charged particles from the Sun, carried by the solar wind, hit Earth's magnetic field, they get pulled toward the poles. These particles collide with molecules from gases like oxygen and nitrogen in the atmosphere, causing them to glow. This creates dazzling light displays called auroras – better known as the Northern and Southern Lights.

Northern Lights

Influential culture and history

The rocky planets are some of our closest neighbours in space – and we've found many ways to connect them to our lives. Whether it's using them to understand our place in the Solar System or imagining what life might be like on these distant worlds, our history and stories are closely tied to the mystery and motions of these planets.

DID YOU KNOW?

The English names for the rocky planets in the Solar System are taken from Roman mythology: Mercury, the messenger god; Venus, the goddess of love; and Mars, the god of war. The exception is Earth, which gets its name from the Old English and Germanic words for 'the ground'.

Wandering stars

The rocky planets, along with Jupiter and Saturn, can be seen with the naked eye. They were called 'wandering stars' in ancient times, and people noticed they seemed to move across the zodiac constellations in the sky. Many cultures believed the planets' positions could predict events and influence people's lives – the practice known as astrology.

Galileo Galilei and his sketches of Venus's phases

Phases of Venus

After the Italian astronomer Galileo Galilei invented the telescope in the 1600s, he began to look at different planets, including Venus. He noticed that Venus went through phases like the Moon and also appeared to change size slightly. This discovery helped prove that Earth was not the centre of the Solar System and changed how people understood space.

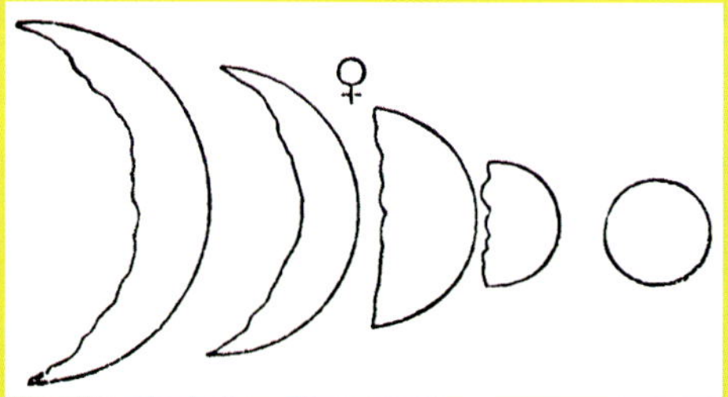

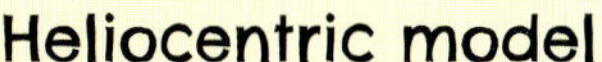

Star of the show

Before the sixteenth century, people widely believed Earth was the centre of the universe. According to this 'geocentric model', the Sun, Moon and planets all orbited around Earth. But as science and technology advanced, astronomers realised that the 'heliocentric model', with the Sun at the centre, was correct. This discovery completely flipped our understanding of the Solar System!

Martian canals

In 1877, an Italian astronomer named Giovanni Schiaparelli peered through his telescope and saw long lines across the surface of Mars. He called them *canali* (Italian for 'channels') – but the similarity of the word to the English 'canals' lead to wild ideas that Martians might have created them. Scientists now know the lines were optical illusions caused by the lenses in the telescope.

Life on Mars?

People have long been fascinated by the idea of aliens from space. Mars has been the most popular planet for imagined life in science fiction, from Marvin the Martian to *War of the Worlds*. Stories have sparked endless speculation about Martians, but so far, we haven't found any signs of life – or even past life – on the Red Planet!

Extraordinary missions

The rocky planets are Earth's closest neighbours, but sending spacecraft to them is no simple task! It takes a diverse and creative group of thousands of people working together to design and build the right technology for the job. By exploring these rocky planets, we can learn more about how our Solar System formed and how Earth has changed over millions of years.

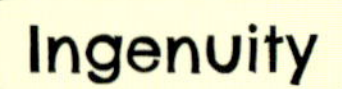

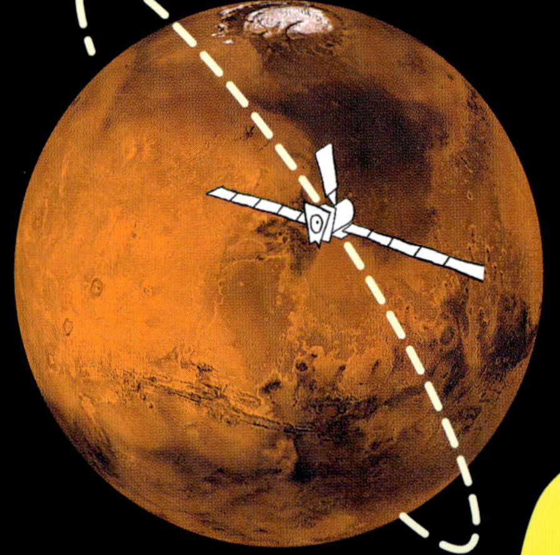

A tricky feat!

Since the 1960s, more than 50 spacecraft have flown by, orbited or tried to land on Mars. With so many missions, it might seem like exploring Mars is easy, but in reality, only about half of them have been successful.

Space blanket

The biggest challenge for ESA's BepiColombo mission to Mercury is protecting the spacecraft from the Sun's intense heat and radiation. A special 'space blanket' – made up of 97 layers of aluminium, plastic and glass ceramic – helps to keep the instruments cool enough to work.

DID YOU KNOW?

The MIXS instrument on the BepiColombo mission, which will help us learn about the types of rocks on Mercury, was built in Leicester, UK.

Looking back at Earth

While many spacecraft and satellites are sent to explore other planets, some stay in Earth's orbit to study our planet. There are more than 1,000 Earth observation satellites, and every day, they send back more than 100 million gigabytes of data – enough to watch 11,500 years of YouTube™ videos!

Surviving Venus

Only a handful of missions have successfully landed on Venus, but they weren't able to operate for very long. The extreme temperature and high pressure on Venus make it difficult for electronics and metals to survive. The Soviet Venera 13 probe, that landed in 1982, lasted for a record-breaking 127 minutes – sending back images and the first recording of actual sounds from another planet!

Perseverance

Out-of-this-world technologies

In 2021, NASA's Perseverance rover landed on Mars to search for signs of ancient life and gather rock samples. This car-sized explorer is like a high-tech laboratory on wheels! It also carried Ingenuity, a small helicopter that proved powered flight on another planet is possible. This technology is now helping scientists design future missions to explore other parts of the Solar System.

Are we there yet?

It's more difficult for an orbiter to reach Mercury than it is to get to Saturn! The Sun's intense gravity makes it difficult for spacecraft to slow down when travelling towards the inner planets. To help, missions use 'gravity assists', which involve using a planet's gravity to adjust their speed. However, this often means taking longer routes, increasing the mission length.

SLOW DOWN

NEXT STOP...
THE GAS PLANETS

Gas Planets

Next stop, the four gas planets orbiting our Sun! These enormous worlds in the outer parts of our Solar System are still relatively unexplored. They inspire curiosity and wonder about what really lies beneath their gassy exteriors!

Jupiter

Everything about Jupiter is huge! It's so vast that all the other planets could fit inside it, with space left over. Massive storms swirl through its atmosphere – some big enough to swallow the entire Earth. Jupiter has many moons, all held in place by the planet's strong gravity, and its magnetic field is so powerful, it reaches all the way to Saturn's orbit.

Quick Facts

Known moons = **95**

Size = **142,984 km in diameter**

Average temperature = **110°C**

Length of rotation = **10.5 Earth hours**

Length of year = **433 Earth days**

Average distance from the Sun = **778 million km or 5.6 AU**

King of the planets

Jupiter is by far the largest of all the planets in the Solar System. In fact, it holds more than 2.5 times the mass of all the other planets put together.

The surface of Jupiter

Zones and belts

As the wax in a lava lamp rises and falls, the gases in Jupiter's colourful atmosphere do the same – creating light and dark bands called zones and belts. The dark belts are caused by gases sinking down and the lighter zones are where gas is rising. These bands flow east and west in opposite directions to each other.

Jupiter and the Galilean moons

Moon dance

The four largest moons of Jupiter – Io, Europa, Ganymede and Callisto – are known as the Galilean moons. Like performers on a stage, the first three moons dance in perfect step with one another. Io completes four orbits of Jupiter in the same time it takes Europa to make two orbits, while Ganymede makes one full orbit.

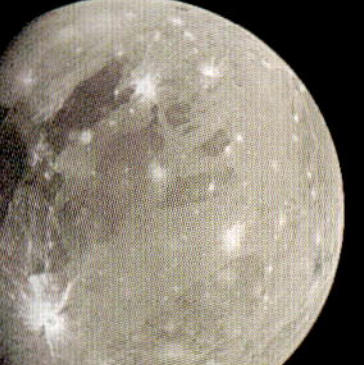

Jupiter missions (launch dates)

Pioneer 10 (flyby) 2 Mar 1972

Voyager 1 (flyby) 5 Sep 1977

Many moons

Jupiter is surrounded by a vast collection of moons, most orbiting far beyond the four Galilean moons. It's likely they formed from captured asteroids or from the remains of ancient collisions. Their numbers have grown so large that scientists give only the most intriguing moons mythological names.

Trojan asteroids

Jupiter shares its orbit with a huge group of asteroids called 'Trojans'. They travel in two packs – one ahead of the planet and one behind. Scientists call them the 'Greek camp' and the 'Trojan camp', named after the two sides of the famous Trojan War in Greek myths.

Light zones

Dark belts

Marzipan smell

Deep within Jupiter's atmosphere, scientists have detected hydrogen cyanide. It's a highly toxic chemical, but it smells like bitter almonds or marzipan!

DID YOU KNOW?

Due to the mainly gas and part-liquid structure of the planet, along with its rapid rotation, Jupiter bulges out at the centre and its poles become flattened as it spins – like how a chef spins pizza dough into a pizza base!

Great Red Spot

Astronomers have been watching the Great Red Spot on Jupiter for more than 150 years. This colossal storm, larger than Earth, rages through Jupiter's upper atmosphere, with winds reaching speeds of up to 400 miles per hour.

Galileo (orbiter) 18 Oct 1989

Ulysses (flyby) 6 Oct 1990

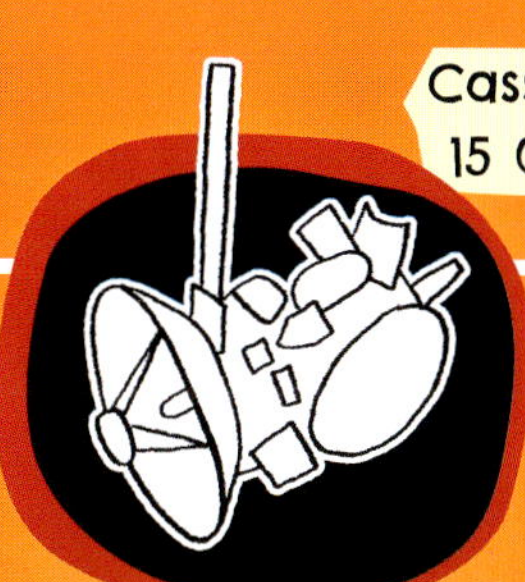

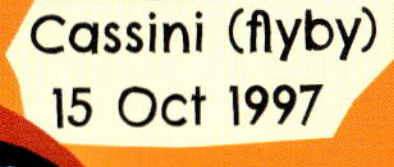

Cassini (flyby) 15 Oct 1997

Juno (orbiter) 5 Aug 2011

JUICE (orbiter) 14 Apr 2023

Saturn

Saturn is close to Jupiter in size, and it also has many moons and powerful storms. But what really makes it special are its dazzling rings. Made of rock and ice, these rings and Saturn's moons move around the planet, just like planets orbit our Sun. In many ways, Saturn's system is like a mini Solar System, and it could hold many clues about how our own Solar System formed.

Quick Facts

Known moons = **274**

Size = **116,500 km in diameter**

Average temperature = **140°C**

Length of rotation = **10.7 Earth hours**

Length of year = **29.4 Earth years**

Average distance from the Sun = **1.4 billion km or 9.5 AU**

DID YOU KNOW?

Saturn is the only planet in our Solar System with a density less than water. This means that if you could find a bathtub big enough, Saturn would actually float on top – just like a giant rubber duck!

Razor-thin rings

Stretching 280,000 kilometres across but only about 1 kilometre thick, Saturn's rings are incredibly thin. If the planet was the size of a basketball, the rings would be 250 times thinner than a human hair! Despite this, the rings shine brightly because they contain chunks of water ice that reflect the Sun's light very well.

Chaotic creation

Saturn's famous rings probably formed from icy comets, asteroids or even moons that broke apart while orbiting the planet. Over time, countless collisions of the debris led to smaller pieces spreading out to create the rings. Another possibility is that an icy moon was shattered by Saturn's powerful gravity as it strayed too close to the planet.

A closer look inside Saturn's rings

Ring rain

Saturn's gravity and magnetic field pull particles from the icy rings towards the planet. Because of this 'ring rain', Saturn loses enough water to fill an Olympic-sized swimming pool every 30 minutes! This means the rings are slowly disappearing and could vanish completely in a few hundred million years.

Polar vortex

One of Saturn's most amazing features is found at its north pole – a massive, hexagon-shaped storm! The Voyager 1 and Cassini missions captured images of this spinning, six-sided vortex – which could never form on Earth. It's about 50 times larger than an average hurricane and nearly twice the width of our planet.

DID YOU KNOW?

Since Saturn has no solid surface, you couldn't land there. But you wouldn't fall straight through either – instead, you'd sink towards the centre, where you'd be crushed and heated by the heavy layers of gas above you.

Saturn missions (launch dates)

Pioneer 11 (flyby) 6 Apr 1973

Voyager 2 (flyby) 20 Aug 1977

Voyager 1 (flyby) 5 Sept 1977

Cassini (orbiter) 15 Oct 1997

Uranus

Uranus really is an oddball planet – from its unusual tilt to its complex atmosphere, extreme seasons and unique moons. Only one spacecraft has ever visited it and much of what we know comes from distant observations. While scientists have uncovered some of its secrets, Uranus remains one of the most puzzling planets in our Solar System.

Quick Facts

Known moons = **28**

Size = **50,724 km in diameter**

Average temperature = **195°C**

Length of rotation = **17 Earth hours**

Length of year = **84 Earth years**

Average distance from the Sun = **2.9 billion km or 0.4 AU**

Miranda

Frankenstein moon

Miranda, one of Uranus's moons, is often called the 'Frankenstein moon' because of its strange, broken-up surface that looks like it doesn't quite fit together. Giant collisions, the strong pull of gravity from Uranus and its other moons, and even icy volcanoes could all have affected Miranda's odd appearance.

Size comparison of Earth and Uranus

Ice

Ice giant

Uranus has the coldest atmosphere of any planet, with temperatures dropping to a bone-chilling -224°C! It's believed there was a collision that knocked the planet onto its side early in the planet's history, which caused some of its heat to escape. Or perhaps something in Uranus's upper layers is preventing the core's heat from reaching the surface. It's still a big mystery!

Sideways world

Uranus spins in a way no other planet in the Solar System does. Its equator is tilted by nearly 98 degrees, making it look as if it's rolling like a barrel through space. Scientists think this bizarre tilt was caused by the same collision that caused the change in temperature. It's likely that the object Uranus collided with was a similar size to Planet Earth.

Discovery

Uranus was the first planet to be discovered with a telescope. It was first thought to be a comet or star when William Herschel observed it in 1781 using his homemade telescope. Herschel also went on to discover two of its largest moons, Titania and Oberon.

Astronomer William Herschel

DID YOU KNOW?

The planet is named after the Greek god of the sky, Ouranos. In Latin, and then later in English, it was spelt as Uranus, giving it a different sound when spoken. However, the correct way to pronounce Uranus is the same as the original Greek name – 'Oo-ra-nus'.

Uranus missions (launch dates)

Voyager 2 (flyby)
20 Aug 1977

Neptune

Neptune, named after the Roman god of the sea, might seem like an inviting watery world. But in reality, it's a dark and icy planet with winds that move faster than the speed of sound and massive storms swirling across its surface. Although Neptune was discovered in 1846, it has only completed one full orbit around the Sun since then. Only a single spacecraft has flown close-by to Neptune, making it one of the most mysterious planets in our Solar System.

Quick Facts

Known moons = **16**

Size = **49,528 km in diameter**

Average temperature = **-214°C**

Length of rotation = **16 Earth hours**

Length of year = **165 Earth years**

Average distance from the Sun = **4.5 billion km or 30 AU**

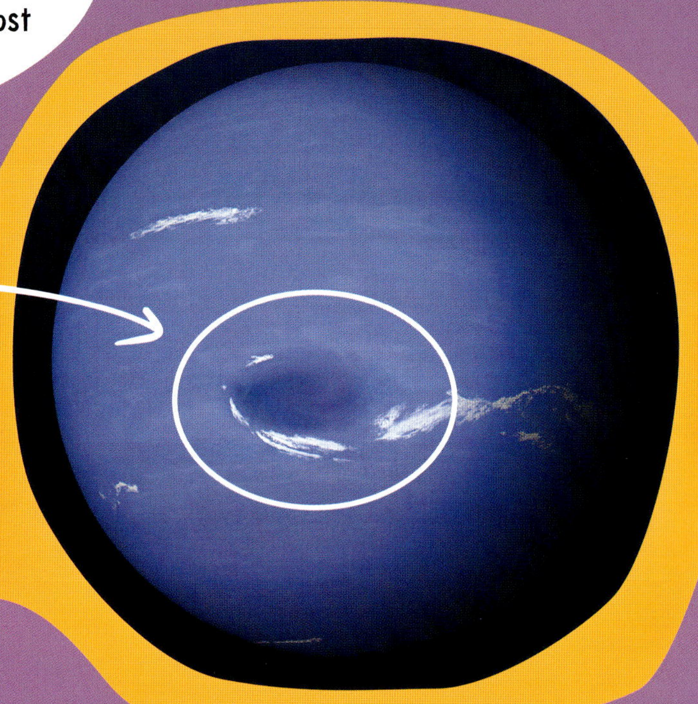

Great Dark Spot

During its flyby in 1989, Voyager 2 spotted a huge dark storm on Neptune called the Great Dark Spot. Since then, the Hubble Space Telescope has observed several more. These 'Great Dark Spots' as they've come to be known, come and go. They swirl around the planet before powerful high-altitude winds tear them apart.

Scooter

The smaller storm next to the Great Dark Spot is called 'Scooter' because it moves so fast across Neptune's surface. The planet's winds are the fastest in the entire Solar System, reaching speeds of more than 2,000 kilometres per hour – nine times faster than the strongest winds on Earth!

Party pooper

Neptune is so far from the Sun that it takes nearly 165 years to complete just one orbit. If we lived there, we'd still grow older, but we'd never live long enough to celebrate even a single birthday.

Adopted moon

Triton is the only large moon in our Solar System that orbits in the opposite direction to how its planet spins. It used to be a dwarf planet in the Kuiper Belt, a region beyond Neptune. But Triton strayed too close to Neptune and was caught by its strong gravity.

Raining diamonds?

There's still a lot to discover on Neptune since it's one of the least explored planets. One exciting idea is that, because of the extreme temperature and pressure, carbon atoms in Neptune's atmosphere might be squeezed into diamonds. This means it might actually rain diamonds there!

Mathematical discovery

Neptune was discovered through maths – the first planet to be found in this way. After the discovery of Uranus, astronomers noticed something odd about its orbit that could only be explained by the presence of another planet. Using mathematical calculations, they worked out where Neptune should be – and in 1846, used a telescope to confirm the discovery.

DID YOU KNOW?

Neptune has a system of rings, just like the other gas giants. However, like Jupiter, Neptune's rings are mostly made of dust, which doesn't reflect much light. This makes them much harder to see.

Neptune missions (launch dates)

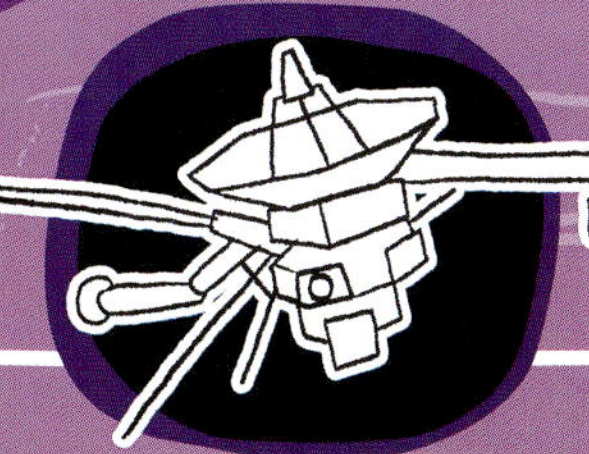

Voyager 2 (flyby)
20 Aug 1977

Fantastic features

Colossal, captivating and full of chaos – that's the best way to describe the gas planets! These giants all have moons, rings, powerful storms and strong magnetic fields, but each one is unique in its own way. And while their thick atmospheres and lack of solid surface mean we could never live on any of them, their exciting features make them fascinating places to explore.

Rings

All four gas giants have rings, but Saturn's are the most famous. They are the biggest and brightest, making Saturn the 'jewel of the Solar System'. It wasn't until the late 1970s that scientists discovered the other gas planets also have rings. They are made of rock, ice and dust, and it's thought they formed from shattered moons or leftover material from the early Solar System.

Cyclones on Jupiter

Storms

Massive storms, similar to giant hurricanes, rage across all the gas giants. The rapid spinning of the planets creates powerful winds that blow in opposing directions. This leads to enormous swirling storms – some of which can last for hundreds of years!

Bright lights

All the gas giants have their own unique light displays called auroras, thanks to their powerful magnetic fields and thick atmospheres interacting with the solar wind. Normally on Earth, auroras tend to be green and red. However, the colours on other planets vary depending on which gases make up their atmospheres.

Aurora on Jupiter

Rock, liquid, gas

There's more to the gas giants than gas! Unlike rocky planets, they don't have a solid surface, so it's hard to say where the atmosphere ends and the planet begins. As you go deeper, the pressure from all the gas above becomes so strong that it turns into liquid. Deeper still, there's a layer of metallic liquid and/or ice surrounding a core, which scientists believe is made of rock and ice.

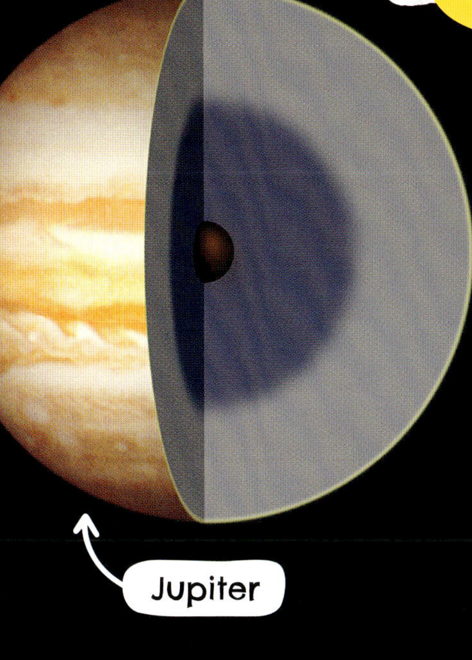

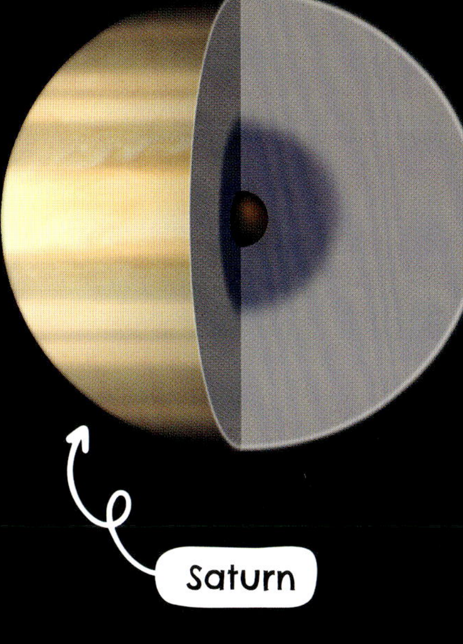

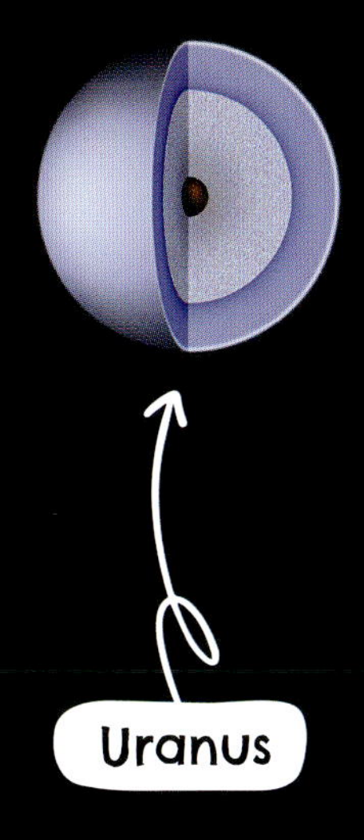

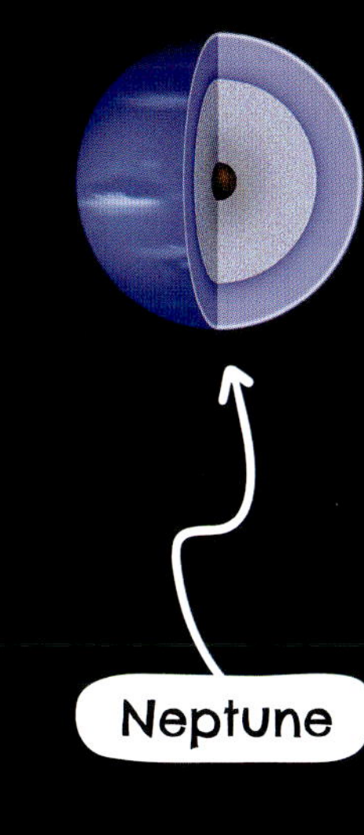

Molecular hydrogen

Metallic hydrogen

Hydrogen, helium, methane gas

Mantle (water, ammonia, methane ices)

Core (rock, ice)

Colourful gases

Gases are usually invisible, but the thick clouds in the gas giants' atmospheres interact with sunlight, giving these planets their colours. On Uranus and Neptune, methane in the upper atmosphere absorbs red light, making them appear blue. Ammonia crystals in Saturn's atmosphere give the planet its soft yellow hue, while Jupiter's shades of white, orange, brown and red come from a mix of hydrogen, helium, water, ammonia and other elements.

Magnetic fields

All four gas planets have strong magnetic fields. Jupiter's magnetic field is so powerful that if we could see it with our eyes, it would appear two to three times larger than the Sun – making it the biggest structure visible from Earth.

Astronomical wonders

The gas giants might seem distant and remote, but certain astronomical events can turn them into headline news. Whether it's a rare lining up of planets or just their usual journey across the sky, these forgotten gems give us amazing chances to admire their beauty.

Venus and the Moon in occultation

Planet party

Although they're millions of kilometres apart, stars, planets and the Moon can appear to move right next to each other in the sky. This is called an 'appulse' or 'close approach'. Occasionally, the Moon can pass directly in front of a planet, making it disappear from view for a while. This event is called a 'lunar occultation'.

Say cheese!

Planets move in different orbits and at different speeds, but sometimes they line up in a special way. When Earth is directly between the Sun and another planet, that planet is said to be 'at opposition'. The planet is closer to Earth than at any other time of the year, making it look bigger and brighter in the sky – a perfect chance for amazing photos!

Dark spot on Jupiter's surface

Pieces of comet P/Shoemaker-Levy 9

DID YOU KNOW?

In 1994, a giant comet called P/Shoemaker-Levy 9 broke into about 20 pieces before crashing into Jupiter's atmosphere. This rare collision left dark spots on the planet for months, which were even more visible than the famous Great Red Spot.

Shifting planets

Long ago, the Solar System was much more chaotic than it is today. Scientists think that as planets began forming 4.5 billion years ago, the cores of Jupiter and Saturn moved closer to the Sun, capturing lots of gas before shifting outwards. And Saturn's gravity may have played a role in flinging Uranus and Neptune outwards to where they are now.

Space vacuums

The gas planets work like giant vacuum cleaners. Their immense gravity sucks in comets and asteroids or sometimes throws them further out into the Solar System. This can help protect smaller rocky planets like Earth. But scientists believe it can sometimes have the opposite effect, sending space rocks hurtling toward those planets instead.

Moon shadows

Over a period of around two weeks, you can watch the Galilean moons complete their orbits around Jupiter. As they pass around and in front of the planet from our view on Earth, they cast shadows on Jupiter's atmosphere. These events can be seen using a good pair of binoculars or a telescope.

Influential culture and history

The outer Solar System has been a place of great discovery. Since ancient times, people have gazed up at the night sky, naming planets and connecting them to their beliefs and cultures. But as science advanced, astronomers discovered huge gas giants and countless moons – adding more vital pieces to the incomplete puzzle of our cosmic neighbourhood.

It's all in the name

When William Herschel discovered Uranus in 1781, he wanted to name it Georgium Sidus – Latin for 'George's Star' – after King George III. But not everyone agreed, and the planet was eventually given the name we use today, Uranus.

Who found Neptune?

The discovery of Neptune was a truly international effort. First, two astronomers – John Adams from Britain and Urbain Le Verrier from France – used maths to calculate where the planet should be. Later, German astronomer Johann Gottfried Galle used these calculations to spot Neptune through a telescope.

Roman connections

Ancient civilisations connected many parts of their lives to their gods and goddesses. They named planets based on their traits – that's why Jupiter, the biggest planet, was named after the chief Roman god. Today, we still see these influences. The month of March comes from Mars, the Roman god of war, and Saturday is named after Saturn, the Roman god of time.

William Shakespeare

I hereby dub thee...

The moons of the gas giants follow unique naming rules. Jupiter's moons are named after the lovers and descendants of the Roman god Jupiter (or the Greek version, Zeus). Some of Saturn's moons are named after the Greek Titan gods and their children. The moons of Uranus are named after characters from the works of Shakespeare and Alexander Pope, while Neptune's moons get their names from Greek and Roman gods of the sea, as well as mythical sea creatures.

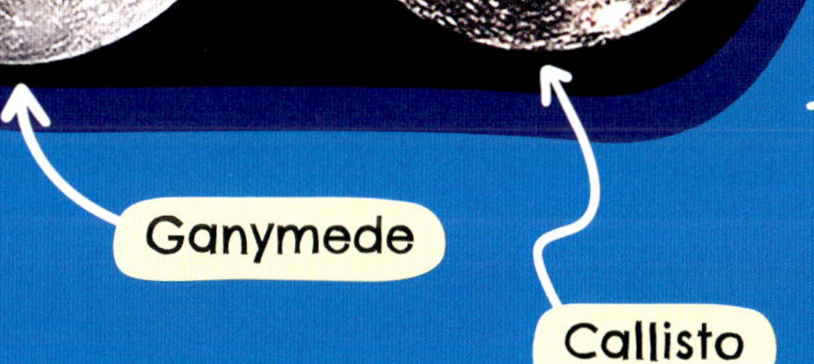

Io

Europa

Ganymede

Callisto

DID YOU KNOW?

In 1610, Italian astronomer Galileo Galilei made an amazing discovery – the first moons beyond our own. Using a telescope he built himself, he spotted four moons orbiting Jupiter – Io, Europa, Ganymede and Callisto. Over several nights, he saw how they appeared to hop across the planet. Today, these four moons are known as the Galilean moons.

3D illustration of Galileo's telescope

King of the moons

For some time, Saturn and Jupiter have been competing for the title of the planet with the most moons. Jupiter briefly took the lead in early 2023, but Saturn quickly snatched back the top spot. With new space missions and advanced technology, astronomers are discovering new moons more often than ever before!

Extraordinary missions

Reaching the gas planets takes years, making space missions long and challenging. This means by the time they arrive, their technology is already old! The further a spacecraft travels, the longer it takes to send and receive messages, so scientists must come up with clever ways to power these spacecraft. The engineering feats that make it possible for us to explore the gas planets are incredible.

James Webb Space Telescope (JWST)

Voyagers 1 and 2

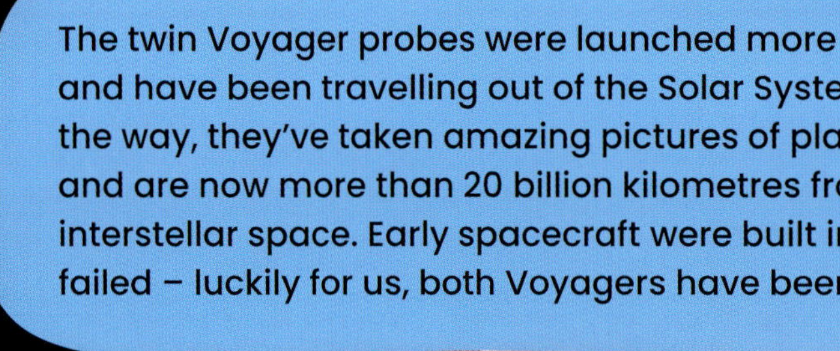

The twin Voyager probes were launched more than 45 years ago and have been travelling out of the Solar System ever since. Along the way, they've taken amazing pictures of planets and moons, and are now more than 20 billion kilometres from the Sun, in interstellar space. Early spacecraft were built in pairs in case one failed – luckily for us, both Voyagers have been a success.

Hubble Space Telescope orbiting Earth

Different views

Astronomers used two powerful space tools – the Hubble Space Telescope and the New Horizons probe – to take pictures of Uranus at the same time. Hubble captured highly detailed images, while New Horizons, 10.5 billion kilometres away, provided a different view. Comparing these images helps scientists to work out what pictures of distant exoplanets might tell us.

Neptune captured by JWST

Neptune's rings

In 2022, NASA's James Webb Space Telescope (JWST) captured the first close-up images of Neptune since Voyager 2 visited in 1989. These amazing pictures showed faint dust rings around the planet – which hadn't been seen in decades!

DID YOU KNOW?

The JUNO probe, which is currently studying Jupiter, has a hexagonal body and three large 'fins' to help it spin like a top, keeping it stable as it zooms around the planet. This spinning motion has the added benefit of allowing its instruments to rotate and face targeted features on the planet as it passes overhead.

JUNO

Cassini-Huygens

Between its launch in 1997 and its fiery plunge into Saturn's atmosphere in 2017, the Cassini-Huygens mission made incredible discoveries. As the first spacecraft to orbit Saturn, it explored the planet's rings, spotted massive storm features and found new moons. It also sent the Huygens probe to land on Saturn's biggest moon, Titan.

JUICE orbiting Jupiter's moons

JUICE

The JUpiter ICy moons Explorer (JUICE) mission launched in 2023, heading towards Jupiter to find out if some of the Galilean moons could support life. To power its journey so far from the Sun, JUICE has huge solar panels – 85 square metres in total! That's about the same area as 12,650 juice cartons stacked together. These are the biggest solar 'wings' ever built for an interplanetary spacecraft.

NEXT STOP... MOONS

Moons

Having visited the eight planets, it's now time to investigate the many moons in our Solar System – starting with our Moon and the missions that have visited it, before heading further out to other weird and mysterious moons. Could we find life in these seemingly extreme locations?

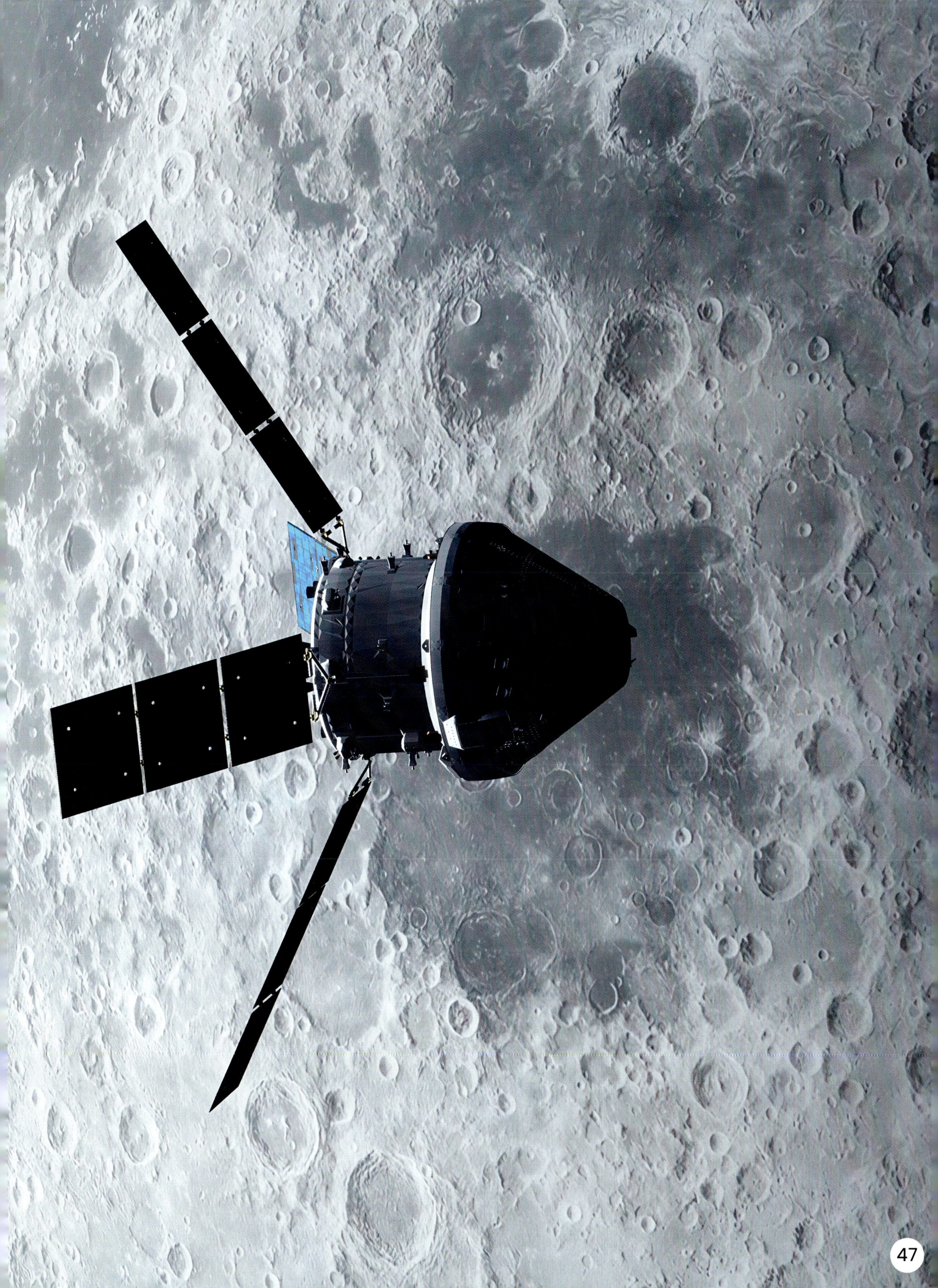

Our Moon

Everyone on Earth can look up and see the bright, shining Moon – no telescope needed! Using just our eyes, we can spot light and dark areas on its surface and watch as its shape seems to change over time. But thanks to modern technology, we can now explore our closest space neighbour in more detail than ever before.

Quick Facts

Average distance to planet = **384,400 km**

Size = **3,475 km in diameter**

Orbit length = **27.3 days**

How far?

The average distance from Earth to the Moon is about 384,400 kilometres – that's far enough to fit 30 Earths in between! But since the Moon's orbit isn't a perfect circle (it's elliptical), this distance changes. Sometimes, the Moon is closer, about 28 Earths away, and other times, it's more distant, around 32 Earths away.

What is the Moon made of?

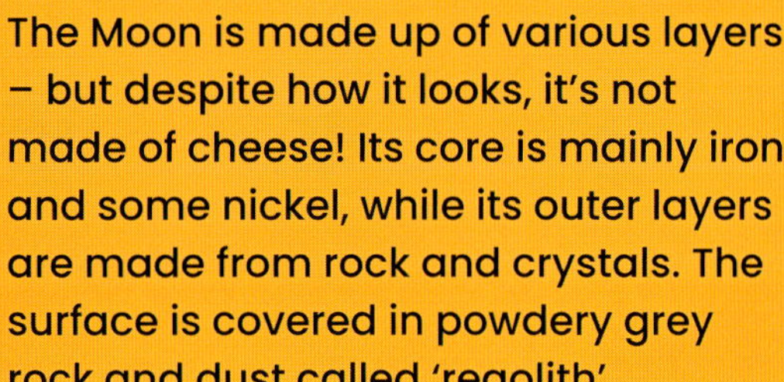

The Moon is made up of various layers – but despite how it looks, it's not made of cheese! Its core is mainly iron and some nickel, while its outer layers are made from rock and crystals. The surface is covered in powdery grey rock and dust called 'regolith'.

The surface of the Moon

A different view

No matter where you are in the world, everyone sees the same shape of the Moon on any given day. But if you're in Australia (in the Southern Hemisphere), the Moon will appear the opposite way up compared to how it looks in the UK (in the Northern Hemisphere).

The Moon as seen from Australia

Tidal locking

Tidal locking is common with large moons, like Earth's Moon. It happens when a moon's rotation matches the time it takes to orbit its planet. This means the same side of the moon always faces the planet.

DID YOU KNOW?

The same side of the Moon always faces Earth because of tidal locking. This means there's a side of the Moon we never see from our planet – called the 'far side'.

Mare Serenitatis

Mare Imbrium

Mare Tranquillitatis

Aristarchus crater

Copernicus crater

Apollo 11 (first crewed mission to the Moon)

Kepler crater

Seas on the Moon

The dark patches on the Moon are called 'maria' – the Latin word for seas. But they're not made of water. These lunar maria were formed long ago from volcanic activity on the Moon when lava flowed into big craters (called basins). Over time, the lava cooled and hardened.

Tycho crater

Dark side of the Moon

The Moon doesn't have a permanent dark side. Half of the Moon is always lit up by sunlight while the other half stays in shadow. The lit and dark areas change throughout the Moon's orbit, but because of tidal locking, we always see the same side from Earth.

The Moon as seen from the UK

Astronomical wonders

The Moon is the second brightest object in the night sky – and sometimes, you can spot it during the day. Its orbit and the way light, which is reflected off the Moon, interacts with Earth's atmosphere can create amazing displays. Some lunar events are rare, but when they happen, they're unforgettable sights!

DID YOU KNOW?

Because of how our brain processes information, the Moon looks bigger when it's just above the horizon than when it's high in the sky. This optical illusion is called the 'Moon Illusion'.

Moon phases

As the Moon orbits Earth, it appears to change shape in the sky – sometimes it looks like a full circle ('full moon'), other times it's a thin crescent ('waxing' or 'waning'), and sometimes it's invisible ('new moon'). But the Moon doesn't make its own light – we see it because sunlight reflects off the Moon's surface! The amount of reflected sunlight we see changes as the Moon moves through its orbit, making it seem as if the Moon is changing shape, but it isn't!

Lunar eclipse

A lunar eclipse takes place when Earth moves between the Sun and the Moon, casting a shadow on the Moon. This can only happen during a full Moon and occurs between two and five times a year. About half of Earth can see a lunar eclipse. During a total lunar eclipse, the Moon appears red to us. This happens because sunlight passes through the Earth's atmosphere and red light gets bent towards the Moon while the other colours get scattered away.

Supermoon

A supermoon happens when a full Moon is at its closest point to Earth in its orbit, called 'perigee'. This makes the Moon look up to 14% bigger and about 30% brighter than when it's furthest away. Supermoons happen three or four times a year.

Moon dogs

On cold nights, moisture in the clouds can freeze into hexagon-shaped ice crystals. These act like glass prisms, bending and spreading moonlight. This creates glowing spots or arcs of light – called 'moon dogs' – beside the Moon, or sometimes just on one side. They can happen at any time of year, although they're more common in winter and when the Moon is full or nearly full.

Once in a blue moon

The phrase 'once in a blue moon' means something that happens rarely, and it comes from a real astronomical event. Normally, we see one full Moon each month because the Moon takes about 29.5 days to go through all its phases. But occasionally, two full moons appear in the same month – at the start and the end, but they don't actually look blue!

Da Vinci Glow

We see 'Earthshine' when sunlight bounces off Earth and lights up the dark part of the Moon. This occurrence, also known as the 'Da Vinci Glow', is easiest to see when the Moon is a thin crescent around the new moon. It's a bit brighter in spring when Earth's tilt and leftover winter ice help to reflect more sunlight.

Extraordinary missions

Many spacecraft – including some of the earliest space missions – have travelled to the Moon. Both robotic and crewed missions have helped us learn more about our closest neighbour in space. Now, in the twenty-first century, more countries and private companies are eager to return and explore it further.

Apollo

In 1969, Neil Armstrong became the first person to set foot on the Moon – making a 'giant leap for mankind'. During the Apollo missions of the 1960s and 1970s, a total of 12 astronauts walked on the Moon and explored its surface, collected rocks, rode lunar buggies – they even played golf.

We have touchdown

Since the 1950s, there have been more than 100 missions to the Moon, both robotic and crewed – but not all have been successful. Reaching the Moon is a challenge, and landing is even trickier! So far, only five countries have successfully made a soft landing – the Soviet Union, the United States, China, India and Japan.

Footprints

The footprints left by Apollo astronauts in the 1960s and 1970s are still on the surface today. That's because there's very little atmosphere to erode them and no wind or rain to wash them away. If you left a footprint on the Moon it would probably still be there in millions of years' time!

Moon missions (launch dates)

- Luna 1-3 (impactor/flyby) 2 Jan-4 Oct 1959
- Zond 3 (flyby) 18 Jul 1965
- Luna 9 (lander) 31 Jan 1966
- Surveyor 1 (lander) 30 May 1966
- Apollo 8-17 (orbiter/lander/sample return) 21 Dec 1968-7 Dec 1972

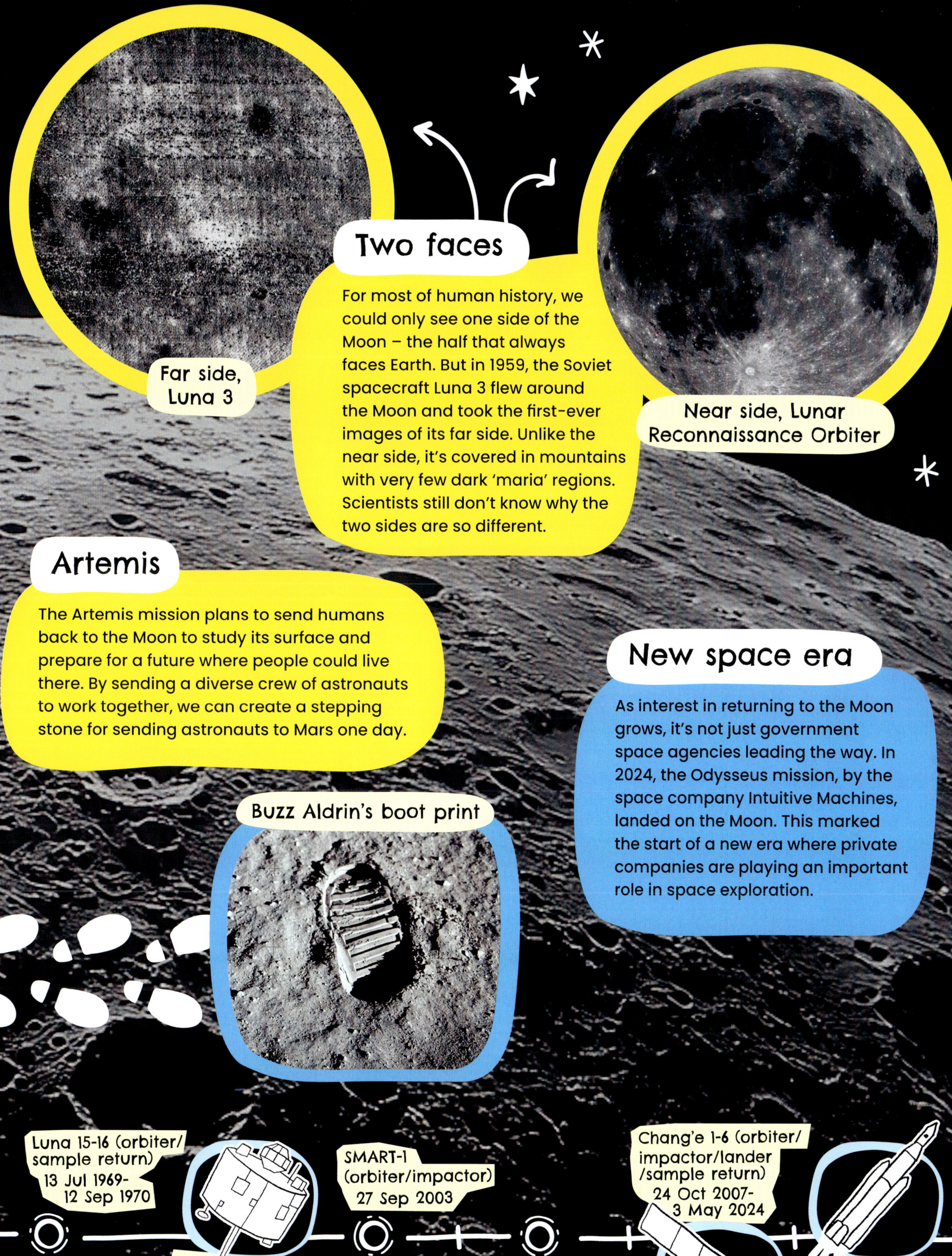

Far side, Luna 3

Two faces

For most of human history, we could only see one side of the Moon – the half that always faces Earth. But in 1959, the Soviet spacecraft Luna 3 flew around the Moon and took the first-ever images of its far side. Unlike the near side, it's covered in mountains with very few dark 'maria' regions. Scientists still don't know why the two sides are so different.

Near side, Lunar Reconnaissance Orbiter

Artemis

The Artemis mission plans to send humans back to the Moon to study its surface and prepare for a future where people could live there. By sending a diverse crew of astronauts to work together, we can create a stepping stone for sending astronauts to Mars one day.

New space era

As interest in returning to the Moon grows, it's not just government space agencies leading the way. In 2024, the Odysseus mission, by the space company Intuitive Machines, landed on the Moon. This marked the start of a new era where private companies are playing an important role in space exploration.

Buzz Aldrin's boot print

Luna 15-16 (orbiter/sample return) 13 Jul 1969-12 Sep 1970

Hiten (orbiter) 24 Jan 1990

SMART-1 (orbiter/impactor) 27 Sep 2003

SELENE (orbiter/impactor) 14 Sep 2007

Chang'e 1-6 (orbiter/impactor/lander/sample return) 24 Oct 2007-3 May 2024

Artemis 1 (flyby) 16 Nov 2022

Influential culture and history

For centuries, people have connected the Moon to their traditions, beliefs and ways of keeping time. Different cultures see unique shapes in the Moon and name it after their lunar gods. Some of the earliest calendars were based on its phases, and many traditions still follow them today. The Moon even influences how some animals navigate and behave.

Moon festival

In Chinese culture, the Full Moon Festival is celebrated with family and friends during the autumn harvest. People gather to enjoy food such as 'mooncakes', and they light lanterns and admire the bright full moon.

A trip to the Moon

Long before humans landed on the Moon, people dreamed of travelling there. One of the earliest films about this idea was *Le Voyage dans la Lune* ('A Trip to the Moon'), made in 1902. It tells the story of explorers who blast off to the Moon in a capsule catapulted from a giant cannon!

Moon-th

The Islamic calendar is based on the Moon's phases, with each month starting when the new crescent moon is spotted. In fact, the word 'month' comes from the word 'moon'!

Usagi

Usagi (oo-saa-gee) the Moon Rabbit is a famous Japanese legend. In the story, a rabbit offers itself as food to a hungry old man – who is actually the Man from the Moon. Touched by the rabbit's kindness, he takes the creature to live on the Moon. Legend has it that you can still see the rabbit's outline on the Moon's surface today.

Leaving the Earth

The first time humans travelled beyond Earth was on Apollo 8, in 1968. Astronauts Frank Borman, Jim Lovell and William Anders looped around the Moon before returning home. During their journey, they took the famous Earthrise photo, showing our planet rising over the Moon's surface. This beautiful image changed how humanity saw Earth and helped inspire people to protect the environment.

Control centre, Apollo 12 launch

There's no 'I' in TEAM

During the Apollo Program, 12 astronauts walked on the Moon – but it took hundreds of thousands of people to make it happen! Around 400,000 people in the United States worked for NASA on Apollo, and many more helped develop the technology and designs that made the missions possible.

It's all in a name

The craters on the Moon are all named after scientists, astronauts, explorers and researchers for outstanding work in their field. For example, in 2018 a crater was named Anders' Earthwise after William Anders and the Earthrise photo he took on the Apollo 8 mission.

Earthrise on 24 December 1968, recorded by Apollo 8

More marvellous moons

It's not just Earth that has a moon – other planets, dwarf planets and even asteroids can have them too! Scientists have already discovered many moons, and there are probably lots more waiting to be found. They come in different shapes, sizes and colours – and their fascinating features make them some of the most interesting places to explore in our Solar System.

Ida

Dactyl

Dactyl

In 1993, Ida became the second asteroid to be visited by a spacecraft when the Galileo probe flew past on its way to Jupiter. Scientists spotted something surprising when they later looked over the images – a tiny moon! This moon, called Dactyl, was the first ever asteroid-moon discovered in 1994. It was named after the Dactyli, mythical creatures from Greek legends who were said to live on Mount Ida.

Volcanic moon

Jupiter's third-largest moon, Io, is tidally locked with its parent planet, meaning the same side is always facing Jupiter – just like our Moon always shows the same side to Earth. But what makes Io exciting is its volcanoes. With more than 400 active ones, it's the most volcanically active place in the entire Solar System!

Io

Double dwarf

Charon, Pluto's biggest moon, is about half the size of its parent dwarf planet and it orbits Pluto once every 6.4 Earth days. In fact, Charon is so large that it's bigger than the dwarf planet Ceres and therefore sometimes Charon and Pluto are known as a double dwarf!

Have you seen a greater crater?

Mimas

Mimas, with its unique oval shape and numerous craters, is the smallest of Saturn's main moons. Its biggest crater, Herschel, makes Mimas look just like the Death Star spacecraft from the film *Star Wars*™!

Quasi-moons

Some objects, like asteroids, can orbit the Sun while keeping in step with a planet. These are called 'quasi-moons'. Although they look like they're orbiting the planet, it's an illusion – they're following their own path around the Sun!

Mini moons

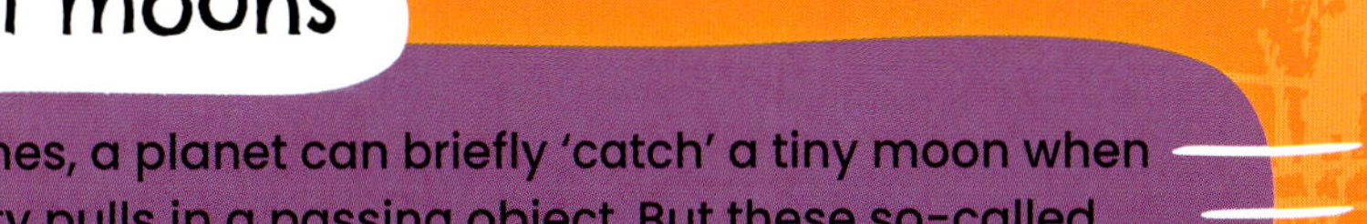

Sometimes, a planet can briefly 'catch' a tiny moon when its gravity pulls in a passing object. But these so-called mini moons don't stay forever – they eventually drift away and continue their journey through the Solar System.

Can you live on a moon?

Earth is the perfect home for life but humans have travelled to and survived on our Moon for only a short time. So would it be possible to live on a moon? There are hundreds of moons in our Solar System – some with water, thick atmospheres or surfaces that look a bit like Earth's. None are exactly like our planet, but could any of them still support life?

Europa

Jupiter's moon Europa might not seem like a place where life could exist. Its frozen surface is constantly hit by radiation from the planet, making it unsuitable for humans. But scientists believe that beneath its icy crust – estimated to be 15–25 kilometres thick – lies a vast ocean of salty water, which could harbour life.

Enceladus

Like Europa, Saturn's moon Enceladus has an icy surface and a salty ocean hidden beneath. But what makes it special are the jets of ocean water it sprays into space! Usefully, this allows spacecraft to fly through the jets and collect samples. So far, tests have shown that Enceladus has all the right ingredients for life.

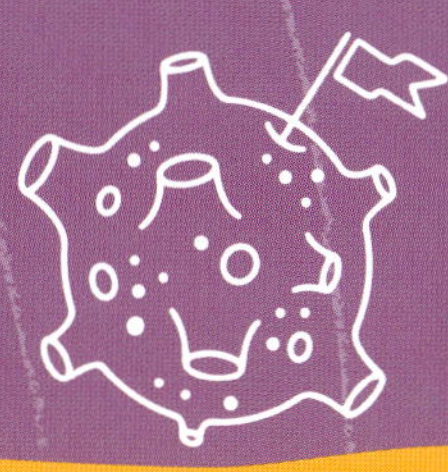

Titan

Scientists are fascinated by Saturn's biggest moon, Titan. It's the only one in the Solar System with a thick atmosphere – made of nitrogen and methane. It even has lakes, rivers and seas! But at -180°C, the liquid isn't water – instead, it's cold enough for methane to exist in liquid form.

Titan's north polar region

Titan in visible light (left) and infrared light without its atmosphere (right)

DID YOU KNOW?

Some scientists believe that there is an underground ocean far below Titan's icy crust – around 100 kilometres down. While Earth-like life might exist there in the salty and ammonia-filled water, life in the rivers and seas on the surface (containing methane and ethane) would be quite different from life on our planet!

Lunar caves

Scientists have discovered caves on the Moon, just like the volcanic caves on the Canary Islands. These deep pits could be entrances to ancient lava tubes – hollow tunnels left behind when molten lava flowed beneath hardened lava. Could these caves be the perfect place for humans to build a settlement?

The Mare Tranquillitatis pit crater on the Moon

Volcanic Cave in La Palma, Canary Islands

Daring moon missions

Because they're so far away, even giant planets look tiny from Earth – and their moons appear even smaller! The best way to explore them is by sending innovative spacecraft, but reaching these distant moons isn't easy. Their low gravity, extreme conditions and long travel times make missions challenging. Scientists must design creative new technology to help spacecraft journey, land and operate safely.

Moon missions (launch dates)

Pioneer 10 (flyby) 2 Mar 1972

Voyager 1 (flyby) 5 Sep 1977

The surface of Titan

Huygens

On 14 January 2005, the Huygens probe made history by touching down on Saturn's largest moon, Titan. It was the first spacecraft to land on a moon in the outer Solar System and the most distant landing from Earth. After a 2.5-hour journey through Titan's thick atmosphere, it reached a solid surface with a soft, sticky mud-like layer underneath – scientists compared it to the dessert crème brûlée!

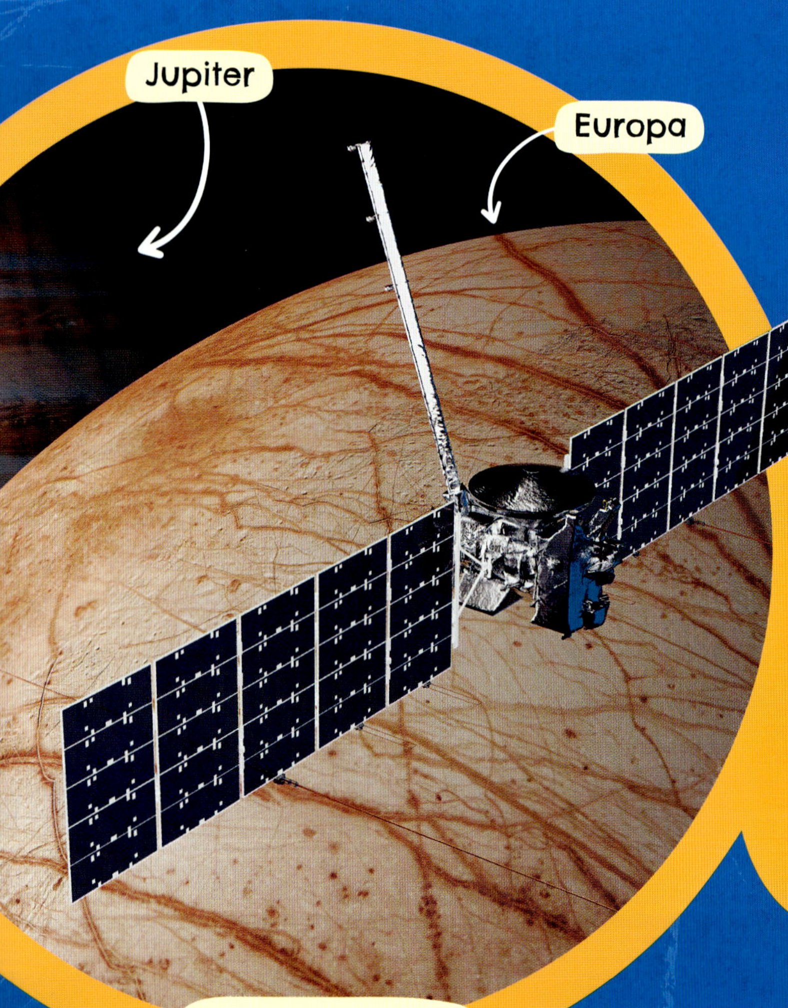

Illustration of the Europa Clipper

Europa Clipper

The Europa Clipper spacecraft – about the size of a basketball court – is NASA's largest planetary explorer ever built. It will fly past Jupiter's icy moon Europa nearly 50 times, mapping the entire surface. Scientists hope this mission will help them find out if Europa has the right conditions for life to exist.

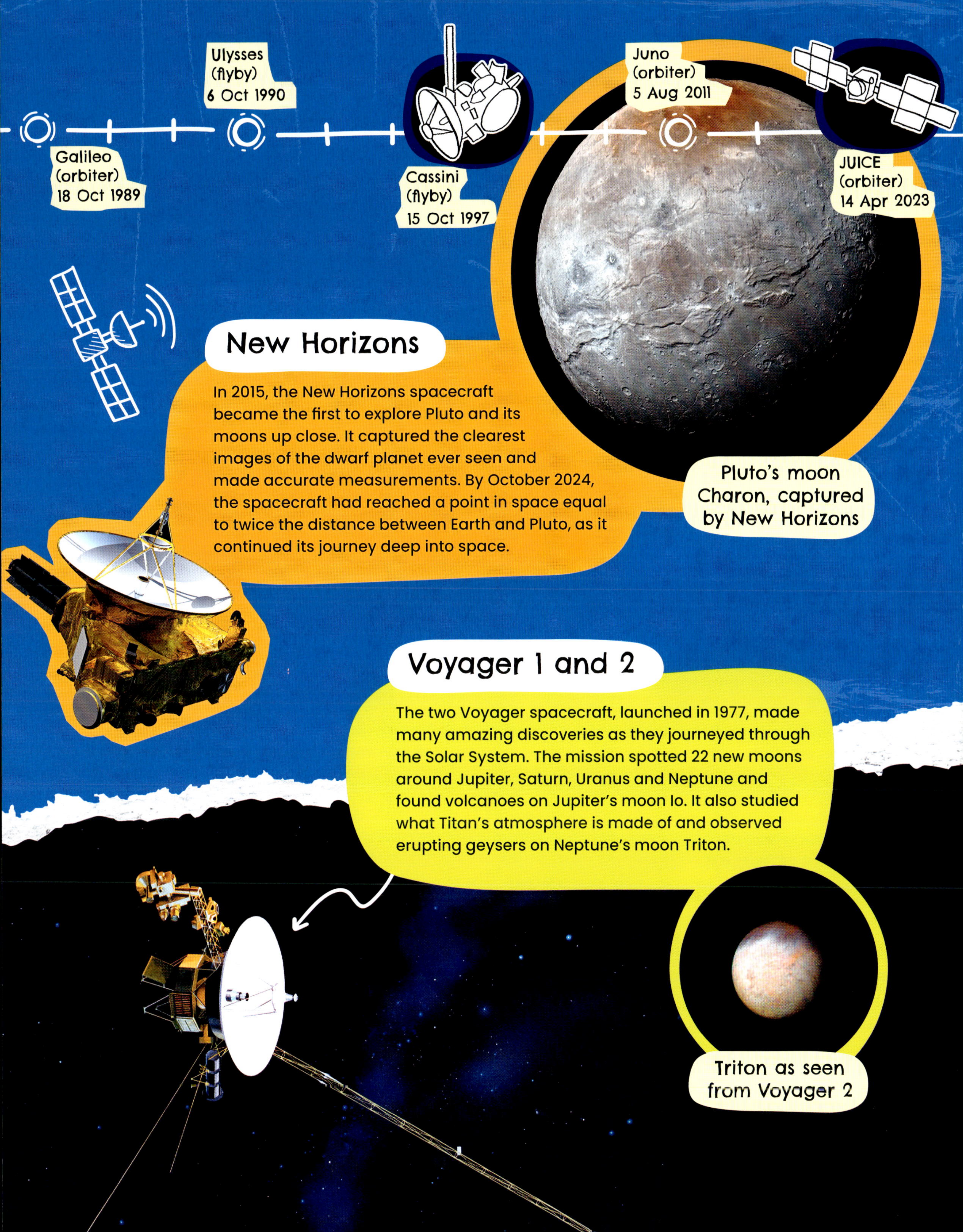

New Horizons

In 2015, the New Horizons spacecraft became the first to explore Pluto and its moons up close. It captured the clearest images of the dwarf planet ever seen and made accurate measurements. By October 2024, the spacecraft had reached a point in space equal to twice the distance between Earth and Pluto, as it continued its journey deep into space.

Pluto's moon Charon, captured by New Horizons

Voyager 1 and 2

The two Voyager spacecraft, launched in 1977, made many amazing discoveries as they journeyed through the Solar System. The mission spotted 22 new moons around Jupiter, Saturn, Uranus and Neptune and found volcanoes on Jupiter's moon Io. It also studied what Titan's atmosphere is made of and observed erupting geysers on Neptune's moon Triton.

Triton as seen from Voyager 2

Fantastic features

The moons in our Solar System formed in different ways and have unique features that give us clues about their history. Many have huge scars from impacts or deep cracks from geological activity. While some moons are round, others have surprising shapes. Like sweets in a pick-and-mix, there's a variety of weird and wonderful moons out there!

Tycho crater

Craters and impacts

Our Moon has almost no atmosphere and no weathering – making it the perfect place to find impact craters. One of the largest and brightest craters is Tycho, found in the Moon's southern region. It's named after the Danish sixteenth-century astronomer Tycho Brahe.

All shapes and sizes

Planets have to be spherical, but there's no such rule for moons. Saturn's tiny moon Pan has a ridge around its equator, making it look like ravioli. Mars's moons, Phobos and Deimos, are covered in craters and have lumpy shapes – like baked potatoes. And Saturn's moon Hyperion, with its deep pits and ridges, looks just like a giant sponge!

Moon maker

Moons form in different ways. Some were once asteroids that got caught by a planet's gravity, while others formed after a massive impact when huge amounts of debris came together. Some moons started as loose space material, pulled in by gravity and slowly clumping together over time. Each moon has a unique story to tell!

Pan

Albedo

We can see moons because they reflect sunlight. The amount reflected is called 'albedo'. Saturn's moon Enceladus has an albedo of 0.99, meaning its icy surface reflects almost 100% of the sunlight that hits it – making it very bright. By contrast, Mars's moon Phobos has an albedo of less than 0.01, making it one of the darkest objects in the Solar System!

Tiger stripes

Near the south pole of Saturn's moon Enceladus, there are four long, parallel cracks in the icy surface known as the moon's 'tiger stripes'. From these giant cracks, jets of water shoot out into space showing that a salty ocean is hidden beneath the ice.

Volcanic moons

Our Moon hasn't had volcanic activity for a long time, but many other moons in the Solar System are still active. Jupiter's moon Io has hundreds of erupting lava fountains that shoot several miles high! Some icy moons around the gas giants, like Enceladus and Titan, have cryovolcanoes – which erupt freezing liquids instead of lava.

NEXT STOP...
SPACE ROCKS

Space Rocks

While there are a handful of planets and hundreds of moons, there are many billions of other 'space rocks' flying around our Solar System. On this leg of the journey, discover the variety of different rocky and icy objects that make space an exciting and lively place!

Asteroids, meteors and meteorites

The leftover scraps from the formation of our Solar System might not seem very interesting at first. However, these space rocks – such as asteroids and meteoroids – help scientists understand how the Solar System has changed over time. Sometimes, these rocks create stunning light displays, while other times, they bring rare space treasures to Earth.

Asteroid family

The small, rocky objects left over from the birth of the Solar System are called asteroids. Most circle the Sun in the main asteroid belt, between the orbits of Mars and Jupiter. Trojan asteroids share an orbit with bigger objects, like planets, but many stray asteroids wander through the Solar System alone. Sometimes, interstellar asteroids arrive as visitors from a distant stellar neighbourhood.

Vesta, the Solar Sytem's second biggest asteroid

Shooting star

If you've ever seen a shooting star, it wasn't actually a star – it was a piece of space rock called a meteor! These rocks have different names depending on where they are. In space, they're called 'meteoroids'. When they enter a planet's atmosphere and burn up, they become 'meteors' (which we see as shooting stars) and if they land, they're known as 'meteorites'.

What's in an asteroid?

Asteroids come in many different shapes and sizes, and can be solid, or more like a collection of loose rubble held together by gravity. What they are made of depends on how far they are from the Sun. Most asteroids closest to the Sun are made of rocks with minerals called silicates. Those further away are more likely to be made of carbon, while a smaller number are made mostly of metal, such as iron or nickel.

433 Eros is made of silicates, nickel and iron

101955 Bennu is made of mostly carbon

Zoomed-in image of pallasites

Types of meteorites

Stony meteorites are the most common type of meteorite forming from the outer mantle of space rocks. Iron meteorites are less common and likely originated in the cores of larger asteroids. Forming where the core meets the mantle are a different type called pallasites – these even rarer stony-iron meteorites have green crystals embedded in them.

Tektites

When a meteorite crashes into a rocky planet, debris is thrown up into the surrounding area. The intense heat from the impact can cause pieces of natural glass to form, called 'tektites'. They are usually the size of a grain of sand and can be black, green, clear, grey or brown.

Zoomed-in image of tektites

Comets

Comets, made of ice, dust and rock, are often called 'dirty snowballs'. Because they formed a long way from the Sun, they have been preserved for billions of years in the freezing outer reaches of the Solar System. They're like time capsules, giving us clues about what the Solar System was like when the Sun was just born.

The main parts of a comet

Comet parts

The nucleus, just a few kilometres wide, is the solid core made of ices, dust and rock. When a comet comes close to the Sun, the ices vaporise creating a hazy cloud of gas and dust around the nucleus – this is the coma. The particles released from the nucleus are pushed back creating two tails – an ion tail made of electrically charged gases and a dust tail.

DID YOU KNOW?

When a solid changes directly into a gas, missing out the liquid stage, the process is called 'sublimation'.

DID YOU KNOW?

A comet's tails don't follow directly behind it like a cat's or a dog's. In fact, the tails face away from the Sun, but the dust tail is also curved as the comet flies through space.

Eccentric orbits

Unlike planets, which travel around the Sun in nearly circular paths, comets have stretched-out, or 'eccentric', orbits. This means they pass very close to the Sun during one part of their journey, then travel far into the outer Solar System before coming back again.

Halley's Comet

Orbit times

Comets that take less than 200 years to orbit the Sun (like Halley's Comet) are called short-period comets. Many of them come from the distant Kuiper Belt region. However, some long-period comets can take millions of years to complete just one orbit. Scientists believe they come from the Oort Cloud, at the very edge of our Solar System.

Oort Cloud

Beyond the Kuiper Belt lies the mysterious Oort Cloud. Scientists believe this vast, bubble-shaped region surrounds the outer edges of our Solar System and is full of icy objects like comets. It is thought to start around 3,500 AU from the Sun and could stretch as far as 100,000 AU!

Kuiper Belt

The Kuiper Belt starts just at the edge of Neptune's orbit, at around 30 AU – 4.5 billion kilometres. It stretches another 20 AU in a bagel-shaped region filled with icy rocks. Even further out is the Scattered Disk, a zone where some objects can be up to 1,000 AU away!

Dwarf planets

Before 2006, the term 'dwarf planet' didn't even exist. The Solar System is a very busy place with lots of different objects within it – so many in fact, that a new category had to be created to separate and identify them from other space rocks. As we continue to make new discoveries, we might find the need to invent new types of categories to classify them.

What are dwarf planets?

Dwarf planets are round, rocky objects that orbit the Sun, but are smaller than Earth's moon. Unlike the major planets, they haven't cleared other similar-sized objects from their path around the Sun. Imagine taking part in a race during sports day – as you race around the track, there are lots of other people running in your lane, so your path isn't clear.

Pluto's story

In 2006, Pluto was reclassified as a dwarf planet by the International Astronomical Union (IAU). Before that, the Solar System was thought to have nine planets, with Pluto as the smallest. But then, scientists discovered other space objects similar in size to Pluto – leading them to rethink what counts as a planet!

Makemake

Haumea

Famous five

The IAU recognises five dwarf planets in our Solar System – Pluto, Ceres, Haumea, Makemake and Eris. Many dwarf planets have moons, and some even have rings. Most of them are found beyond Neptune's orbit, but Ceres is in the asteroid belt between Mars and Jupiter.

Named by an 11-year-old

When Pluto was discovered, it was initially given the name Planet X. But its current name was actually suggested by an 11-year-old girl named Venetia Burney, after she'd been reading about Greek and Roman legends in children's books. She thought the Roman God of the underworld, Pluto, was a good name for this distant and dark planet.

Minor planets

Besides the eight planets and numerous comets, most other small objects orbiting the Sun are called 'minor planets'. This group includes dwarf planets, asteroids and distant space rocks beyond Neptune – known as trans-Neptunian objects (TNOs).

Eris

Pluto

DID YOU KNOW?

There are probably hundreds more dwarf planets in our Solar System waiting to be discovered and confirmed. Some possible candidates include Gonggong, Sedna, Orcus and Quaoar – which was spotted to have a ring around it!

Exoplanets

Imagine if every star in the Milky Way had at least one planet orbiting it – that would mean there could be 100 billion planets in our galaxy alone! Planets that orbit outside of our own Solar System are called exoplanets. So far, we've only found a few thousand, but they show that our Solar System is pretty unique. Exoplanets come in all shapes and sizes – the hope is that one day, we might find an Earth-like one!

Types of exoplanets

There are four main types of exoplanets – Earth-like rocky planets, gas giants, Neptunian and super-Earths. In our Solar System, the four inner planets are rocky, while the four outer planets are gas giants. Super-Earths are exoplanets bigger than Earth but smaller than gas giants, while Neptunian exoplanets are similar in size to Uranus and Neptune.

The Goldilocks Zone

When scientists search for exoplanets, one of the key questions is: could any of them support life? To be like Earth, a planet must be in the 'Goldilocks Zone' – the perfect distance from its star. If the planet's too far away, it's too cold, but if it's too close, it's too hot. The right distance depends on the type of star the planet orbits.

Just right!

Multiplanetary systems

Multiplanetary systems (those with more than one planet) might not be rare – we just don't have the technology to find them easily. So far, scientists have only found one exoplanet system with eight planets like ours – Kepler-90. All its planets orbit closer to their star than Earth does to the Sun. Another exciting system is TRAPPIST-1, which has seven planets. Four of them are in the Goldilocks Zone, where conditions could support life.

Exoplanets in the Kepler-90 System

Kepler-90b
Kepler-90c
Kepler-90i
Kepler-90d
Kepler-90e
Kepler-90f
Kepler-90g
Kepler-90h

What did you call me?

Exoplanet names might seem odd, but they follow a pattern. The first part is related to the star's discovery. It can start with the star's name, like Proxima Centauri, or it's named after the telescope that found it. For example, Kepler-90 is the 90th star found by the Kepler Telescope. The second part identifies the exoplanet. It is a lowercase letter that shows the order in which the exoplanet was discovered.

Exoplanet detectives

Exoplanets are really hard to find because they're small, far away and don't produce their own light. Astronomers use special techniques to spot them. One way is the transit method – which means watching for repeated tiny dips in a star's brightness as an orbiting exoplanet passes in front of it.

Lost in space

Sometimes an exoplanet gets thrown out of its star system and becomes a rogue planet. If it happens to pass in front of a bright object, scientists might notice a brief dip in light – but the exoplanet will probably never be detected again!

DID YOU KNOW?

Our closest exoplanet is Proxima Centauri b, a super-Earth just four light-years away. That might sound close, but even the fastest thing we know – light – takes four years to get there. If we used the fastest spacecraft we have today, it would take around 80,000 years!

Illustration of the surface of Proxima Centauri b

Fantastic features

Some massive, landscape-altering events have shaped incredible features on space rocks in our Solar System. On the other hand, natural forces such as gravity have created simpler but still fascinating formations. These space rocks hold clues that help us understand our place in the Universe.

Craters on Earth

Throughout Earth's history, there have been collisions with asteroids and comets. However, it can be hard to find evidence of these impacts because wind, rain and movement in Earth's crust (tectonic activity) have worn them away. Some craters are still visible, though, such as the famous Barringer Crater (also called Meteor Crater) in Arizona, USA. It's about 1.2 kilometres wide and 180 metres deep.

Barringer Crater
Arizona, USA

Pluto's heart

In Pluto's distant past, a violent collision with another small world left it with a huge basin that quickly filled with nitrogen ice. This created its famous heart-shaped feature, Tombaugh Regio. During the day, some of the ice turns into gas, then re-freezes back into ice at night. This heartbeat-like cycle drives nitrogen winds around Pluto.

Can you see it?

Ancient rocks

There are two types of stony meteorites – chondrites and achondrites. Achondrites come from objects such as planets and moons, where heat has separated their materials into layers. Chondrites contain tiny round particles called chondrules, which haven't changed since they first formed. That makes them the oldest rocks you can ever touch – about 4.5 billion years old!

Chondrite

Comet 67P Churyumov-Gerasimenko

Size matters

Planets are usually bigger than the Moon, which in turn is larger than dwarf planets. Asteroids tend to be smaller than dwarf planets, and comets smaller still. Since most comets are only a few kilometres wide, they don't have enough gravity to pull themselves into a round shape. That's why Comet 67P Churyumov-Gerasimenko looks a bit like a rubber duck!

Weird and wonderful

With so many exoplanets, it's no surprise that they have many strange environments. Some have furious winds with raining glass that would cut you to shreds, and others are made of diamond on the inside. There are even exoplanets that are darker than the blackest lump of coal, and some with sizzling surfaces hotter than many stars. We're discovering new worlds all the time – who knows what other weird and wonderful exoplanets we'll find in the future.

Astronomical wonders

Space is always in motion and constantly changing, producing incredible sights for us to witness today, or uncover from the past. Some events caused by space rocks, like meteor showers, can be seen with the naked eye every year. Others need the world's most powerful telescopes - and perfect timing - to catch them.

Meteors

When bits of space rock enter our atmosphere, they burn up, creating bright streaks of light called meteors. Meteors that are random and unpredictable are known as sporadic meteors. But they can also appear together in greater numbers as part of an annual event called a meteor shower.

Meteor showers

As comets (and sometimes asteroids) orbit near the Sun, they leave behind trails of debris. Every year, as Earth circles the Sun, it passes through these debris trails and causes a shower of meteors to appear in the sky. These meteor showers happen at roughly the same time each year, making them exciting to try and spot!

Annual meteor showers

Name	Peak date	Constellation	Rate
Quadrantids	3–4 January	Bootes	80-120
Lyrids	22–23 April	Lyra	15-20
Eta Aquariids	5–6 May	Aquarius	Up to 50
Perseids	12–13 August	Perseus	Up to 100
Draconids	8–9 October	Draco	Up to 5
Orionids	21–22 October	Orion	Up to 20
Leonids	17–18 November	Leo	Up to 10
Geminids	13–14 December	Gemini	Up to 150
Ursids	22–23 December	Ursa Minor	Up to 10

Keywords:

Constellation = meteor showers are named after the constellation that the meteors appear to come from in the sky

Rate = the rate of a meteor shower is how many meteors you're likely to see in one hour in ideal conditions

Perseid meteor shower

Geminid meteor shower

DID YOU KNOW?

Pluto takes 248 years to orbit the Sun, and for 20 of them, it moves inside Neptune's orbit. But don't worry – the two planets will never crash into each other! That's because Neptune goes around the Sun three times for every two times Pluto does, keeping them safely apart.

Glowing comets

Comets are usually dark and hard to see. But when they get close to the Sun (called 'perihelion'), they heat up and produce their long, beautiful tails – and we can spot them in the sky. Depending on their path and how close they are to Earth, comets can be visible for weeks or months before they disappear again.

Periodic comets

Name	Orbital period	Year of next close approach
2P/Encke	3.3 years	2027
67P/Churyumov–Gerasimenko	6.45 years	2028
55P/Tempel–Tuttle	33 years	2031
1P/Halley	75–76 years	2061
109P/Swift-Tuttle	133 years	2126
C/1995 O1 (Hale-Bopp)	2,534 years	4385

Influential culture and history

Space rocks existed long before humans – and have left their mark on centuries of civilisation. Earth carries the scars of past impacts, ancient chronicles describe bright events in the sky, and modern entertainment brings the excitement of imaginary distant worlds to life.

Bayeux Tapestry

Throughout history, people from different cultures believed that comets were omens of bad luck or disaster. One of the most famous examples is in the Bayeux Tapestry, which shows a comet streaking across the sky while people point and stare in amazement.

What's that?

Bayeux Tapestry

Exoplanets in Hollywood

Although the first exoplanet was discovered in 1992, science fiction imagined them long before that. In the 1977 film *Star Wars*™, George Lucas created Tatooine, an exoplanet orbiting two stars. Movies like *Avatar* have also explored exoplanets, with its story set on Pandora, a moon orbiting the fictional planet Polyphemus.

The Great Bombardment

About four billion years ago, many scientists think Earth went through a period called the 'Great Bombardment'. Towards the end of this period, lots of asteroids and comets crashed into our planet. It's thought these space rocks may have brought the building blocks for life, such as water and amino acids, to Earth.

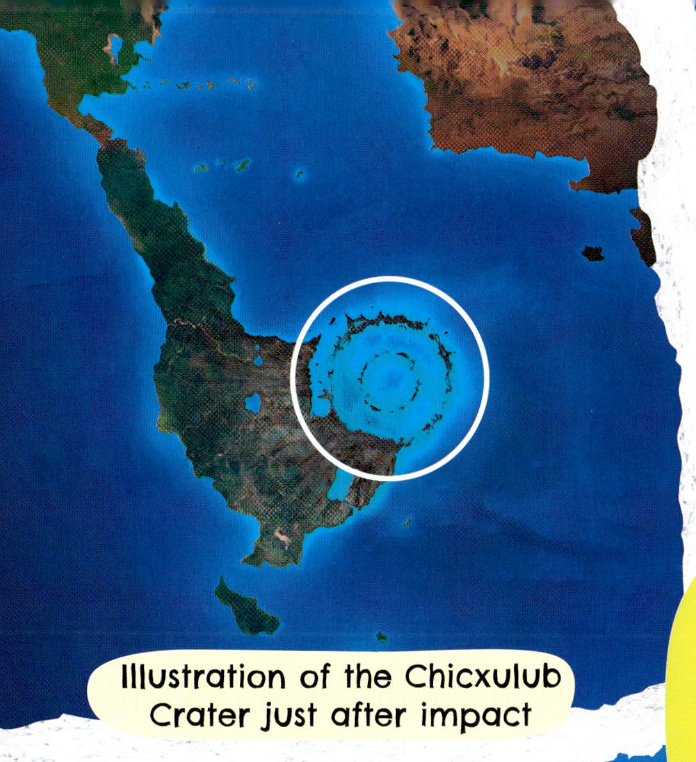

Illustration of the Chicxulub Crater just after impact

Dinosaur extinction

The Chicxulub Crater, located off Mexico's coast, formed when a massive asteroid struck Earth around 65 million years ago. Scientists believe this was a contributing factor in the demise of the dinosaurs. Setting off a chain reaction, this huge blast sent debris and dust into the atmosphere, blocking sunlight and stopping plants from growing. With less food, herbivores struggled, which then affected the carnivores – leading to the extinction of these land-dwelling creatures.

Barwell – the Christmas meteorite

On Christmas Eve 1965, a meteorite – the biggest ever recorded in Britain – fell on the village of Barwell. It was about the size of a turkey and broke into pieces as it crashed. One fragment dented a car, and the owner threw away the debris, not realising what it was. Later, when he tried to claim insurance, the company called it 'an act of God' and refused to pay!

Hello again!

Comet Encke

Campo del Cielo meteorite at the National Space Centre, Leicester

Field of the Sky

The heaviest collection of iron meteorites was discovered in Argentina, near Buenos Aires. In an area called Campo del Cielo – meaning 'Field of the Sky' – a weight of nearly 100 tonnes of meteorites was found scattered across at least 26 small craters.

Rediscovered comet

The shortest period comet that we know is called Comet Encke and was named after Johann Encke in 1819. It takes just 3.3 years to complete an orbit of the Sun. Generally, if you are the first to observe a comet you are able to name it, but Johann Encke wasn't the first to observe this comet. It was 'discovered' every 3.3 years by a different astronomer until Encke predicted this was the same returning comet and therefore it became named after him.

Extraordinary missions

Some of the most daring space missions target the smallest objects. Reaching, orbiting and even landing on tiny space rocks is extremely difficult because of their low gravity – and observing these miniature bodies is also very tricky since they are so far away. But thanks to advanced technology, scientists have created incredibly sensitive tools that help us to explore these distant worlds.

New Horizons

DID YOU KNOW?

The Hayabusa mission, from the Japanese space agency JAXA, was the first to successfully return a sample from an asteroid (25143 Itokawa) to Earth.

Slingshot

To reach faraway Pluto, the New Horizons spacecraft used Jupiter's gravity to give it a massive speed boost. By slingshotting around the gas giant, it reached an incredible speed of 83,000 kilometres per hour! This shortened its journey from 15 years to just 9.

Comet selfies

The ESA mission Rosetta was the first spacecraft to orbit a comet, sending a lander, Philae, to explore its surface. After a bumpy landing in 2014, Philae sent back the first-ever photos from a comet's surface.

Game, set, samples!

In 2006, the Stardust mission became the first spacecraft to return samples from a comet back to Earth. The spacecraft used a tennis racquet-sized collector tray covered in an aerogel, which acted like a sponge to absorb the dust and debris from the tail of Comet Wild 2.

Space rocks missions (launch dates)

Stardust (flyby & sample return) 7 Feb 1999

Hayabusa 1 & 2 (orbiter & sample return) 9 May 2003 & 3 Dec 2014

Rosetta-Philae (orbiter & lander) 2 Mar 2004

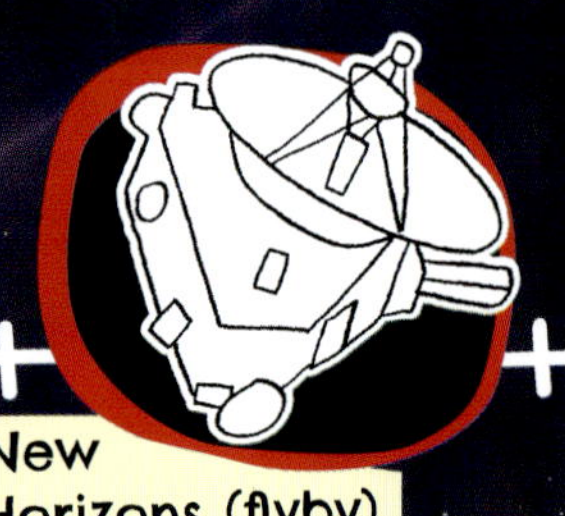

New Horizons (flyby) 19 Jan 2006

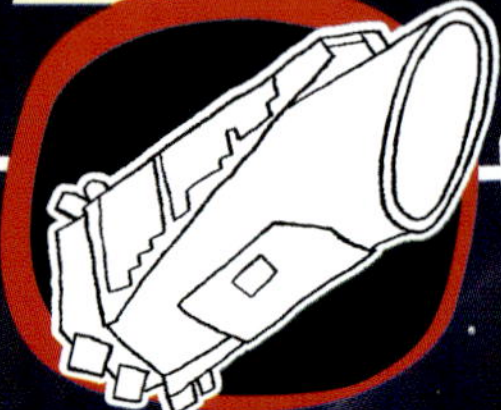

Kepler (orbiter) 7 Mar 2009

Discovering exoplanets

The Kepler telescope watched more than 150,000 stars in a small patch of the sky, looking for repeated dips in their brightness – signs that an exoplanet might be passing in front of them. During its nine-year mission, Kepler discovered thousands of exoplanets – including some Earth-sized planets that might be habitable.

Kepler on its K2 mission

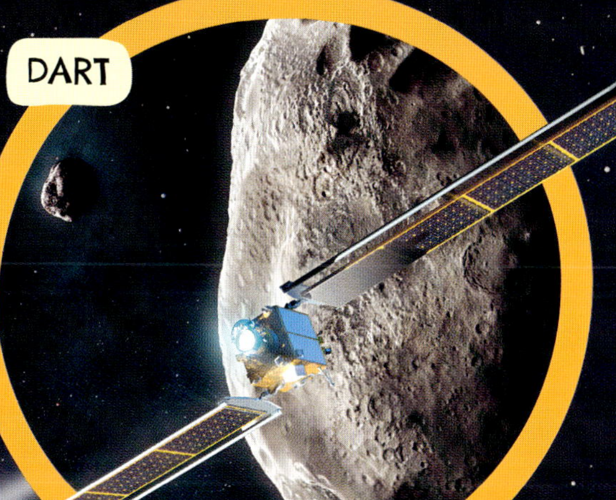

Sample return

In 2023, NASA's OSIRIS-REx spacecraft brought back samples from asteroid Bennu. Containing some of the oldest material in the Solar System, Bennu could help scientists learn how the Solar System formed – and maybe even reveal clues about the origins of life on Earth.

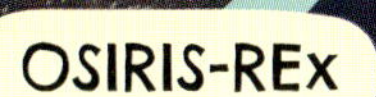

Asteroid impact

The DART (Double Asteroid Redirection Test) mission was designed to test whether crashing a spacecraft into an asteroid could change its path. About the size of four washing machines, DART smashed into the asteroid Dimorphos in 2022, successfully altering its orbit around a larger asteroid. This technology could one day help protect Earth from a dangerous collision.

NEOWISE (orbiter) 14 Dec 2009

OSIRIS-REx (orbiter & sample return) 8 Sep 2016

Lucy (flyby) 16 Oct 2021

DART (impactor) 24 Nov 2021

Psyche (orbiter) 13 Oct 2023

NEXT STOP... STARS

Stars

Get ready to uncover the secrets of our star, the Sun. It is a great example of an average star, but there are an astronomical number of stars in the Universe. By studying lots of different types of stars, we can learn more about the changing nature of the cosmos.

What is a star?

Stars are like twinkling jewels in the night sky, but they are much more than the tiny points of light we see from Earth. They vary in size, colour and age. Since stars live for millions to trillions of years, scientists can't observe a single star's entire lifetime. However, by studying a variety of stars in space, they can piece together how stars change over time.

Messier 41

Giant ball of plasma

Atoms are the basic building blocks that make up practically everything around us. An atom is made of tiny particles. At the centre is the nucleus, which contains protons and neutrons. Electrons move around the nucleus. When an atom is heated to very high temperatures, some of its electrons break free, turning it into a plasma. All stars are made of this plasma, or superheated gas.

Atom turning into plasma

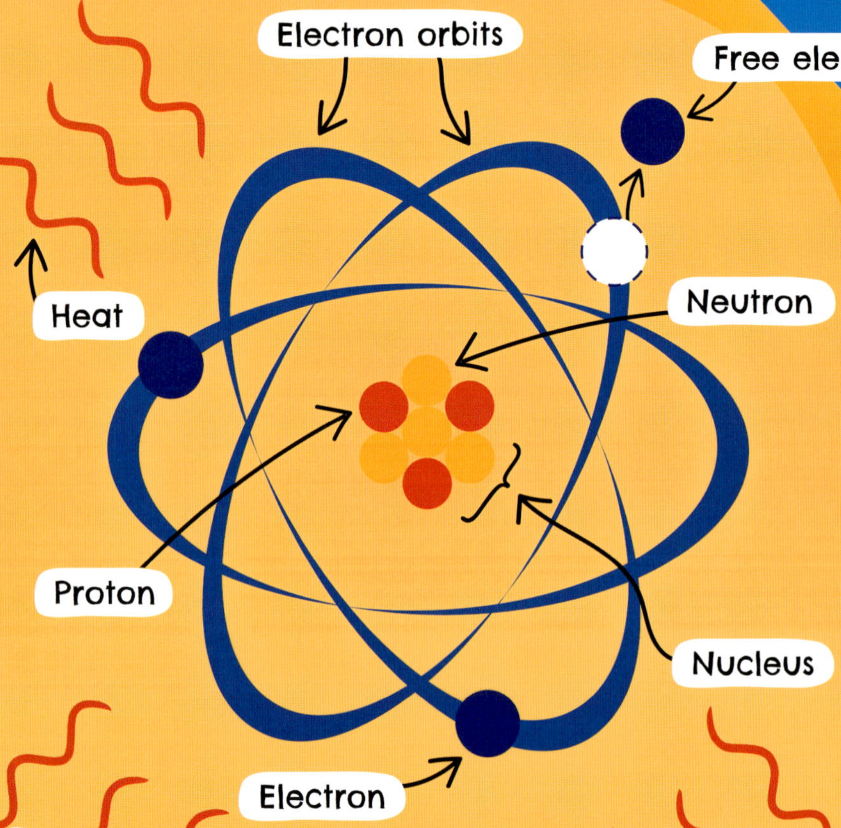

Nuclear fusion

Fusion is the process of joining two things together – like squishing two balls of clay into one. At the centre of a star, it is the nucleus of one hydrogen atom that fuses with another. In the process, energy is released and it is this 'nuclear fusion' that powers a star.

Star power

Even though most gases are invisible, we can see stars because because they release light and heat energy. The Sun sends an incredible 44 quadrillion joules of energy to Earth every second – that's as much energy as around 44 million large electric power plants would produce!

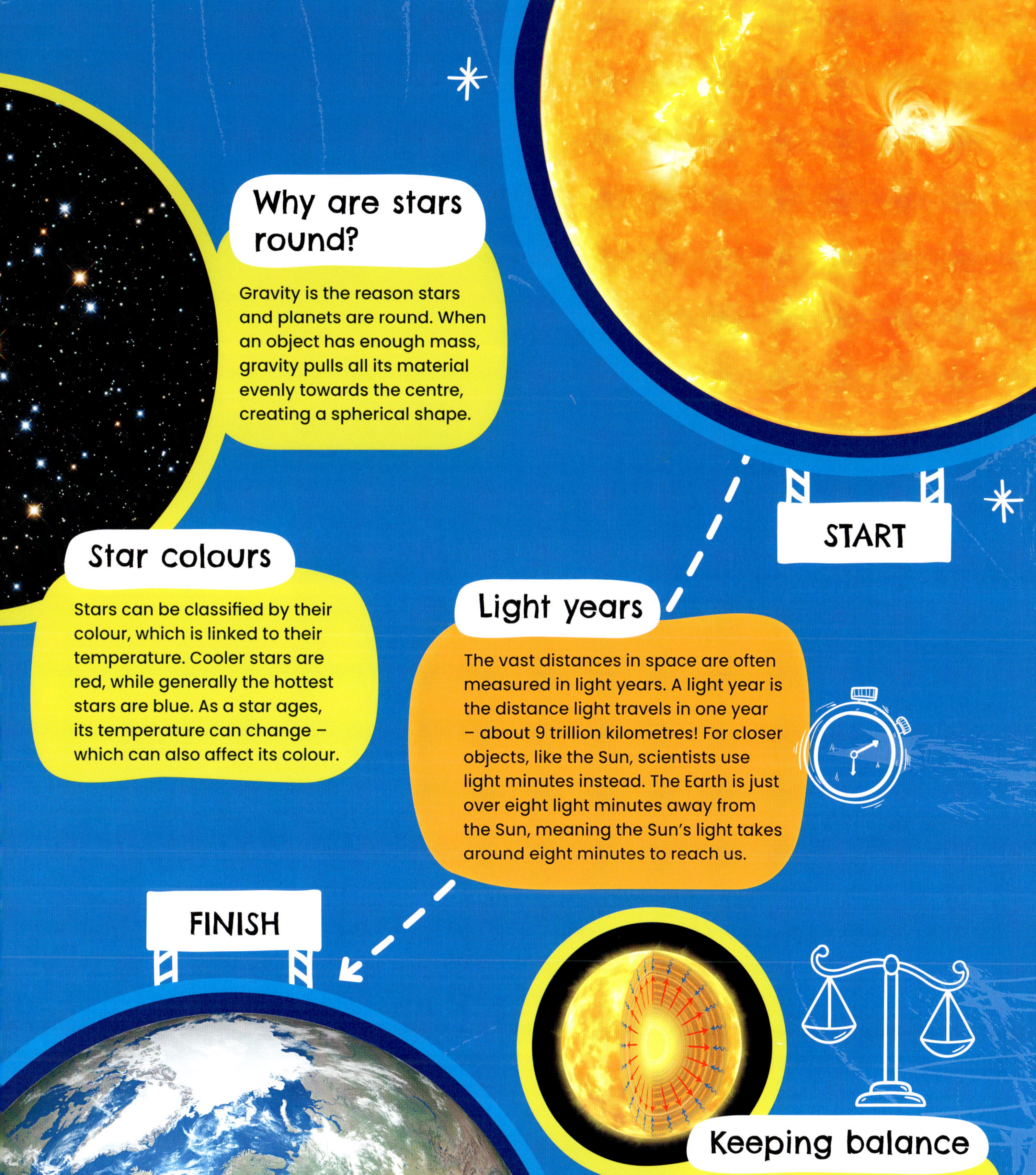

Why are stars round?

Gravity is the reason stars and planets are round. When an object has enough mass, gravity pulls all its material evenly towards the centre, creating a spherical shape.

Star colours

Stars can be classified by their colour, which is linked to their temperature. Cooler stars are red, while generally the hottest stars are blue. As a star ages, its temperature can change – which can also affect its colour.

Light years

The vast distances in space are often measured in light years. A light year is the distance light travels in one year – about 9 trillion kilometres! For closer objects, like the Sun, scientists use light minutes instead. The Earth is just over eight light minutes away from the Sun, meaning the Sun's light takes around eight minutes to reach us.

Keeping balance

Stars are always trying to remain in balance. The energy from nuclear fusion pushes outwards, while gravity – which holds the star together – pulls inwards. When these forces become unbalanced, the star moves to the next stage of its life cycle.

The Sun

Our Sun shows just how powerful and massive stars can be. Even though it's much closer to us than any other star, its light still takes over eight minutes to reach us! In that time, it travels across a vast expanse of space to heat and light up our planet. The Sun's energy is essential for life, providing the warmth and light that make Earth a place where living things can thrive.

Quick Facts

Size = **1.4 million km in diameter**

Visible surface temperature = **5,500°C**

Core temperature = **15,000,000°C**

Length of day = **25 Earth days at the equator; 36 Earth days at the poles**

MeGAStar

The Sun is mostly made of hydrogen gas – about three-quarters of it. The rest is mostly helium, with tiny amounts of other elements like oxygen, carbon and nitrogen. Hydrogen is the Sun's main fuel, and even though it consumes around 600 billion kilograms of it every second, it still has enough to last another 5 billion years or so.

Day and night

All the planets in our Solar System have day and night because they spin on their axes. When a planet faces the Sun, it's daytime, and when it turns away, it's nighttime. The length of a planet's day depends on how fast it spins and how much it tilts on its axis.

Solar energy

The Sun is our main source of energy, and people have learned how to use this power in clever ways! Solar panels soak up sunlight and turn it into electricity. This energy can be used for heating, cooking and powering our devices. The Sun is a 'renewable' energy source, which means it won't run out.

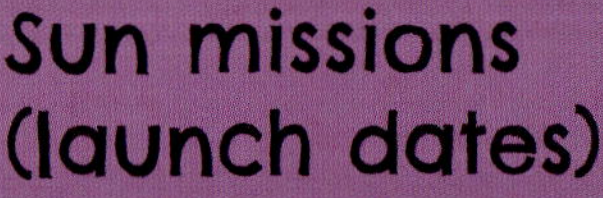

Sun missions (launch dates)

- Ulysses (orbiter) 6 Oct 1990
- Wind (orbiter) 1 Nov 1994
- SOHO (orbiter) 2 Dec 1995
- ACE (orbiter) 25 Aug 1997
- Hinode (orbiter) 23 Sep 2006
- STEREO (orbiter) 25 Oct 2006

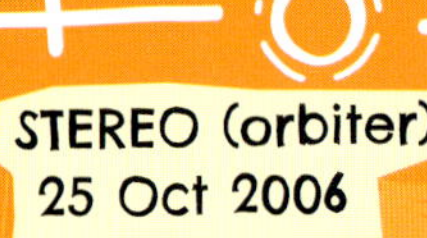

Sunspots

Sunspots are dark spots – a bit like freckles – that appear on the visible surface of the Sun (known as the photosphere). These cooler regions give off less light and therefore look darker. The spots form in places where the Sun's magnetic field is strong, which stops the heat from reaching the surface.

DID YOU KNOW?

The Sun is 4.6 billion years old – the same age as the Solar System – and is only halfway through its life cycle. Scientists think Earth is half a million years younger than the Sun.

Types of stars

We can classify stars based on their colour, size and life stage. By studying different kinds of stars, astronomers can build a picture of star populations and learn more about how they are born, how they change over time and what happens when they die.

Red dwarfs

Red dwarfs are thought to make up 75% of the Milky Way's stars. They are the smallest and coolest type of stars. Because of this, they take a long time to burn their fuel, so they can live for an incredibly long time – in fact, some are thought to have lifespans that are longer than the current age of the Universe.

AU Mic

Yellow dwarfs

Stars like our Sun are known as yellow dwarfs or G-type stars, but the Sun is an average-sized star compared to others in the Universe. These types of stars have a lifespan of around 10 billion years. These stars might be average in size and temperature but scientists think they are likely to outshine 90% of the stars in the Universe.

The Sun

2MASSJ22282889-431026

Brown dwarfs

When an object in space is bigger than a planet but not big enough to become a star, it is called a 'brown dwarf'. These objects are usually 10 to 80 times the mass of Jupiter, but they can't squeeze the material in their cores enough to start nuclear fusion. Because of this, they are sometimes called 'failed stars'.

Blue giants

Blue giant stars are some of the largest and hottest stars in the Universe. They have more than twice the mass of our Sun, but because of their intense heat and large size, they continuously use up huge amounts of energy. This means they have a much shorter lifespan than other stars – around 10 million years.

AG Carinae

White dwarfs

White dwarfs are created after a star like our Sun has used up its fuel. At the end stage of a small star, its outer layers are pushed out into space, while the inner parts are pulled tightly, leaving behind a hot core called a 'white dwarf'. These stars are incredibly dense, squeezing the mass of an entire star into an object about the size of a planet.

A white dwarf star in the Hyades star cluster

R Sculptoris

Red giants

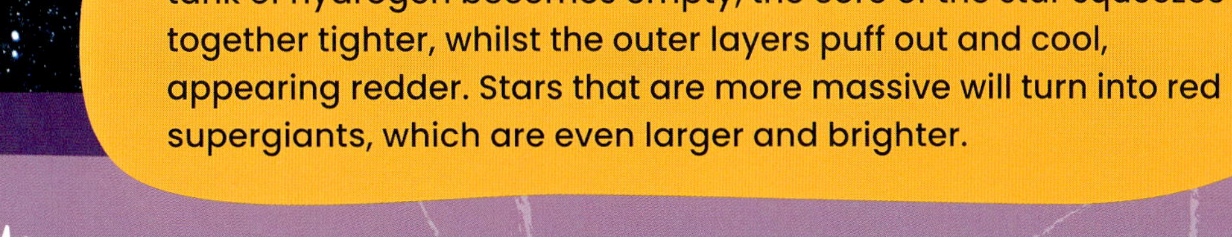

Identified by their large size and cooler surface temperature, red giants are stars in the later part of their lives. When a star's fuel tank of hydrogen becomes empty, the core of the star squeezes together tighter, whilst the outer layers puff out and cool, appearing redder. Stars that are more massive will turn into red supergiants, which are even larger and brighter.

Life cycle of a star

People have been looking up at the same stars for generations – and that might make you think they last forever. But just like people, stars have a lifespan – although they can live for millions, billions or even trillions of years! During that time, they go through different stages. By studying stars at different points in their life cycles, scientists can also learn more about the elements that make up everything around us.

DID YOU KNOW?

When the Sun runs out of hydrogen fuel in about 5 billion years, it will expand into a red giant star. It will swell up, becoming so big that it will engulf Mercury and Venus. It might even swallow Earth too!

Stellar nebula

Low- and medium-mass stars (generally red dwarfs and yellow dwarfs)

Red giant

High-mass stars (generally blue giants)

Red supergiant

Made of stardust

In the Universe's early history, there was mostly just hydrogen and helium. The first stars fused these light elements into heavier ones, throwing them out into space when they died. Our Solar System was formed from this material, meaning the carbon, oxygen, nitrogen, calcium and phosphorus in your body were created inside a star. We are all made of stardust!

Light and heat

For most stars, the hotter they are, the brighter they shine. However, some stars don't follow this pattern. For example, white dwarfs are very hot but not very bright.

Beginnings and endings

Nebulas are giant clouds of gas and dust that are the birthplaces and graveyards of stars in our Universe. They come in many different shapes and sizes. Some are many times larger than our Solar System and can be seen in the night sky, sometimes with the naked eye. One of the most famous is the Orion Nebula, which is found in the middle of the pattern of stars, or asterism, called Orion's Sword.

DID YOU KNOW?

Neutron stars are what's leftover when a massive star ends its life. When the star's fuel runs out, it collapses in on itself violently and rebounds in a supernova explosion. A teaspoon of material from a neutron star would be roughly 900 times the mass of the great Pyramid of Giza!

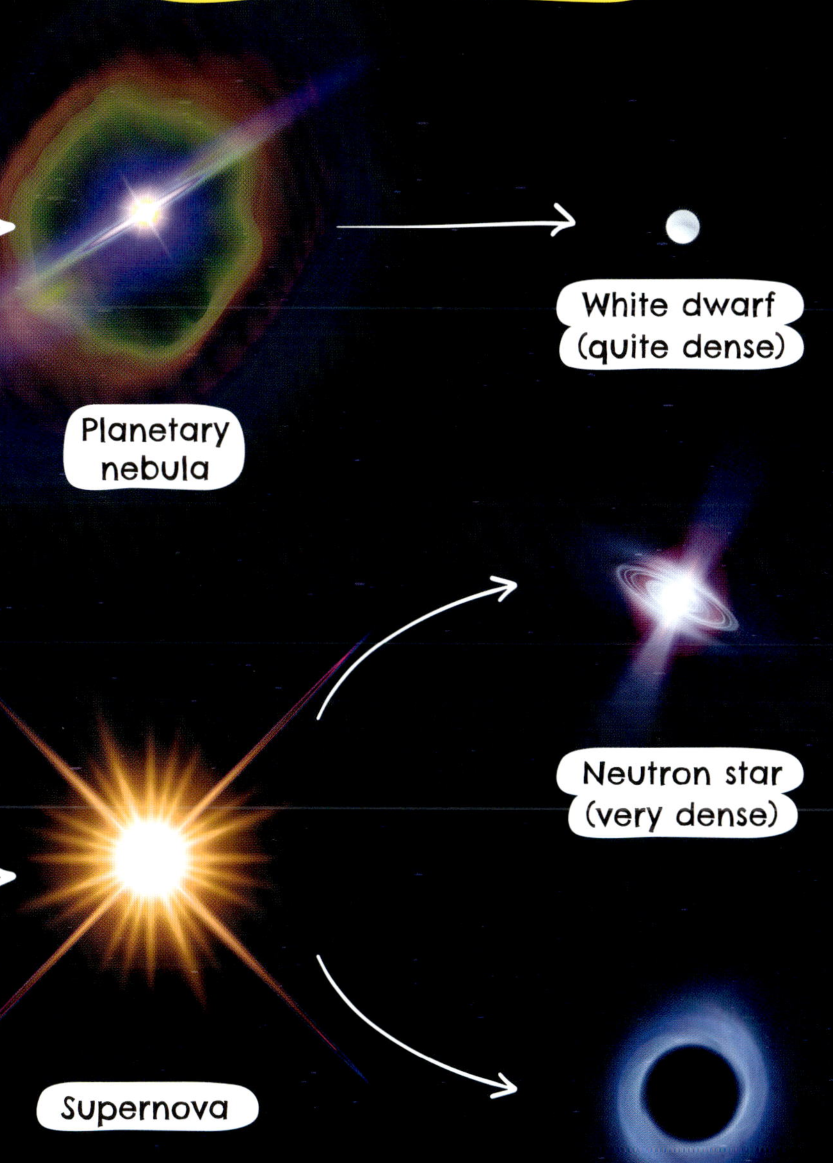

Great recyclers

At the end of a star's life, its material is flung back into space as a planetary nebula or in a supernova explosion. Over time, this expelled gas and dust can come together to form a dense cloud or nebula where new stars are born, starting the process all over again – it's the Universe's way of recycling!

Black holes and supernovas

Black holes are areas of space with such intense gravity that even light, the fastest thing we know, cannot escape. They usually form after a supermassive star dies, creating a supernova explosion. Black holes are difficult to see, but astronomers can work out their location by observing how nearby stars move under the gravitational force of these invisible objects.

Fantastic features

Stars are incredibly active and display many beautiful features. Their mass, temperature and energy output are invisible to the human eye, but the laws of physics help us understand them. The Sun, our closest star, has many features that show us just how dynamic and powerful stars can be.

Dimming stars

Stars that regularly dim and brighten are known as variable stars. This can happen when a brown dwarf orbiting a star blocks some of its light, or when the star's surface layer expands and contracts. Some stars even dim just before they explode in a supernova!

Betelgeuse is a star that brightens and dims

Twinkle twinkle little star

Because stars are so far away, they appear like points in the sky. As their light travels through Earth's turbulent atmosphere, it becomes bent and distorted. So, to our eyes, the stars seem to twinkle. Brighter stars appear to shimmer more – this is why Sirius, the brightest star in the night sky, twinkles so much!

Sirius shining brightly above the alpine mountains

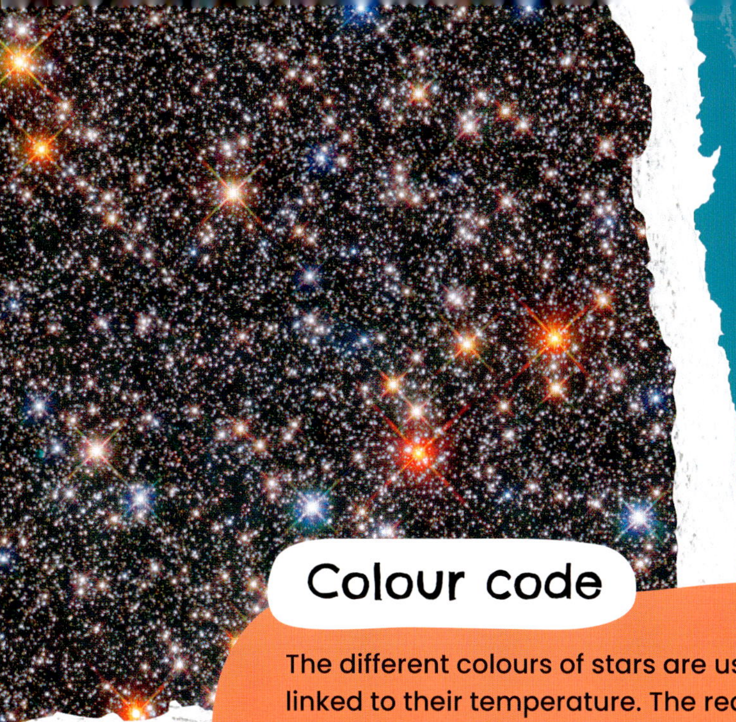

Solar prominence

A solar prominence is a dense cloud of plasma that reaches outwards from the Sun's surface. It can form in just a day but can last for months, stretching hundreds of thousands of kilometres into the Sun's outer atmosphere, the corona.

Colour code

The different colours of stars are usually linked to their temperature. The redder the star, the cooler it is, and the bluer the star, the hotter it is. Because blue light carries more energy than red light, a star needs to be much hotter to glow blue. It's similar to heating metal – at first, it glows red, but as it gets hotter, it turns blue.

Blacksmith working with hot metal

Why are there no green stars?

Stars emit a range of colours, but our eyes blend them together. When a star emits mostly green light, it also shines with a lot of red and blue light. Our eyes combine these colours, making the star look white. This is the case for our Sun.

DID YOU KNOW?

Hotter than the surface of the Sun, the outer atmosphere around the Sun is known as its corona. It's not usually visible because of the brightness of the Sun but reaches temperatures of over 1 million degrees Celsius.

Solar eclipses

Solar eclipses are thought to be bad omens by some people and others see eclipses as amazing, rare events not to miss. They happen when the Moon, as it orbits around our planet, passes between the Earth and Sun, blocking out our star's light. We get different types of solar eclipses depending on the positions of the Sun, Earth and Moon.

A total eclipse in Texas, USA (Apr 2024)

Sun

Umbra

Earth

Moon

Penumbra

Total eclipse

During a total solar eclipse, the Moon completely blocks the Sun, creating a full shadow called the 'umbra'. This happens about every 18 months, but it isn't visible everywhere in the world. If you're lucky enough to be in the right place, you'll see only the Sun's outer atmosphere, the corona. This amazing sight can last up to 7.5 minutes – but remember, never look directly at the Sun!

Partial eclipse

A partial solar eclipse happens when the Sun and Moon are not perfectly lined up. This makes the Sun look crescent-shaped as the Moon partially passes in front of it. The effect is caused by the Moon casting a wider and fainter shadow, called the 'penumbra', on Earth.

A partial eclipse in Leicester, UK (Mar 2025)

An annular eclipse in Singapore (Dec 2019)

Annular eclipse

As the Moon orbits Earth, its distance changes. When it's further away from Earth and passes in front of the Sun, it doesn't completely block the Sun's light. Instead, we see a bright ring – called an 'annular solar eclipse' or a 'ring of fire' – appear around the Moon.

DID YOU KNOW?
Even though the Moon is about 400 times smaller than the Sun, it appears just the right size to completely cover it during a total eclipse, as it's about 400 times closer to Earth than the Sun is.

DID YOU KNOW?
At the start and end of the moment of total eclipse, a dazzling spot of light can be seen coming from the Sun and its corona. This creates the stunning effect of a diamond ring in the sky.

Cool view!

Eclipse shadow

A solar eclipse is an amazing sight from Earth, but from space, it looks quite different. As the Moon blocks the Sun's light, it casts a shadow on Earth – and this is what you'd see. Anyone within this shadowed region on Earth would be able to view the solar eclipse.

The Moon's shadow seen from the ISS

Safety first!

The Sun is extremely bright and should never be looked at directly. Even during a solar eclipse, when most of the Sun is blocked, just a glimpse of sunlight can damage your eyes. To watch safely, use specially designed eclipse glasses or a solar filter on a telescope. You can also cast an image of the eclipse using a pinhole projector or even a colander!

Astronomical wonders

From exploding stars and expanding clouds of stardust to powerful bursts from the Sun and spectacular polar light shows, stars create incredible cosmic events. As huge energy sources in the Universe, they can change their appearance, affect their surroundings, and even leave lasting impacts beyond their own solar neighbourhoods.

DID YOU KNOW?

The Sun's corona constantly emits solar wind – streams of charged particles – in all directions. These particles travel vast distances at high speeds, reaching up to three times beyond Pluto's orbit.

Solar cycle

Every 11 years, the Sun's magnetic field flips from north to south. This causes quiet periods of low activity, called 'solar minimum', and times when the Sun is most active, known as 'solar maximum'. Solar maximum happens halfway through the cycle and can be tracked by monitoring sunspots on the Sun's surface.

Auroras

When the particles from the Sun reach Earth's magnetic field, they are pulled towards the North and South poles. There, they collide with gases like oxygen and nitrogen, creating beautiful light displays called auroras. In the Northern Hemisphere, they are known as the Aurora Borealis, while in the Southern Hemisphere, they are called the Aurora Australis.

Aurora Borealis in the Arctic

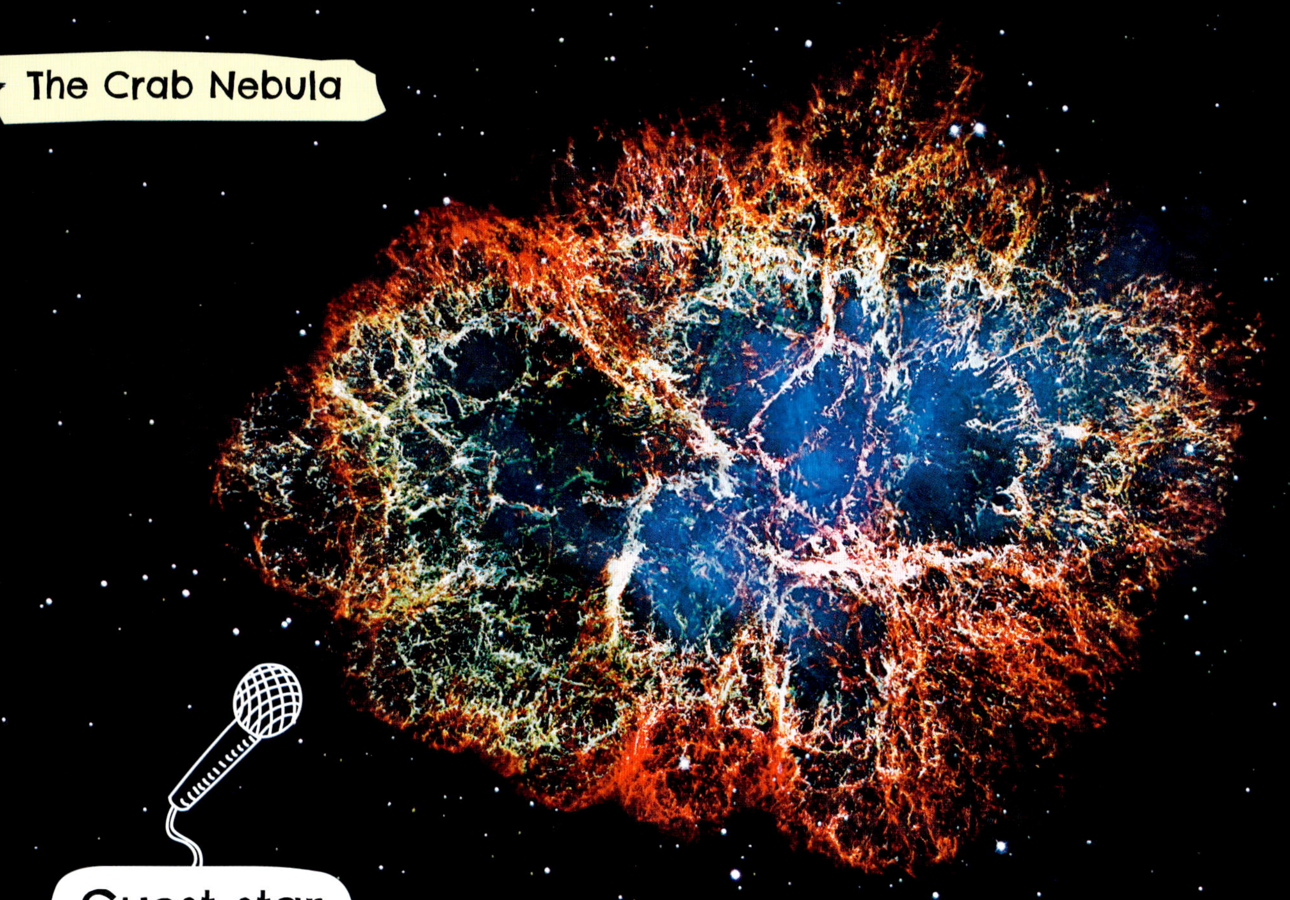

Guest star

In the year 1054, Chinese astronomers observed a bright new star in the sky. This 'guest star' was actually a supernova explosion, temporarily shining so brightly that it was visible during the day for several weeks. Today, in the constellation of Taurus, we can still see the remains of this supernova, known as the Crab Nebula.

Planetary nebula

When a low- to medium-mass star reaches the end of its life, it sheds its outer layers and forms a beautiful planetary nebula. The light of the white dwarf left at the centre energises the chemicals in this cloud of gas and dust, causing it to glow in different colours. When our Sun dies, it will also form a planetary nebula.

Solar explosions

Both solar flares and coronal mass ejections (CMEs) are huge explosions from the Sun, but they are slightly different. Solar flares happen when energy is suddenly released creating a giant burst of light. CMEs are instead enormous clouds of plasma that are flung out into space.

Orion

Betelgeuse

Just like volcanoes and earthquakes on Earth, scientists can't predict exactly when a star will explode. Betelgeuse, a red supergiant in the constellation Orion, is nearing the end of its life and is expected to explode soon – though that could mean within the next 1,000 years or even up to 100,000 years!

Constellations

It's easy to join bright stars dot-to-dot to create patterns, known as constellations. Although stars do move, their positions in the sky don't change for very long periods of time, so people have used the same constellations for thousands of years. No doubt, ancient seafarers used constellations to help them find their way, and today, scientists use them to help locate astronomical objects in space.

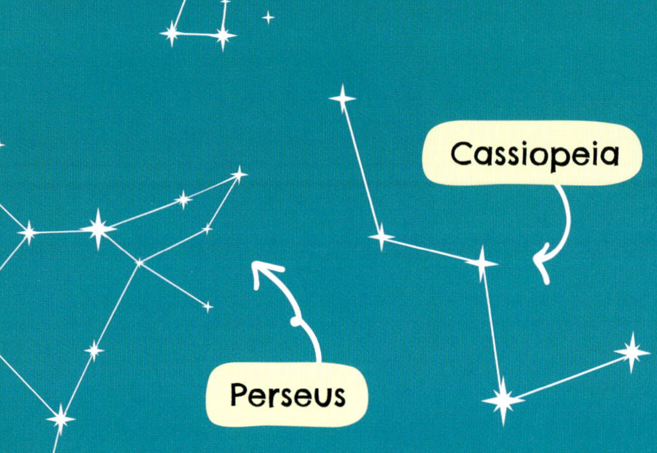

How many are there?

Different cultures and countries around the world have their own constellations, but not everyone agrees on them. The International Astronomical Union (IAU), a leading authority on astronomy, recognises 88 official star patterns. These are used by scientists and astronomers across the world.

Circumpolar stars

Stars closest to the North Star (also known as Polaris) that remain above the horizon at all times are known as circumpolar stars, so they can be seen all year long! In the UK, this includes the stars in the constellations of Cassiopeia, Draco and Perseus.

Circumpolar star trails in the northern sky

DID YOU KNOW?

For centuries, the Plough asterism has been used for navigation and can help point to Polaris. This star is directly above the North Pole and can be used to find north.

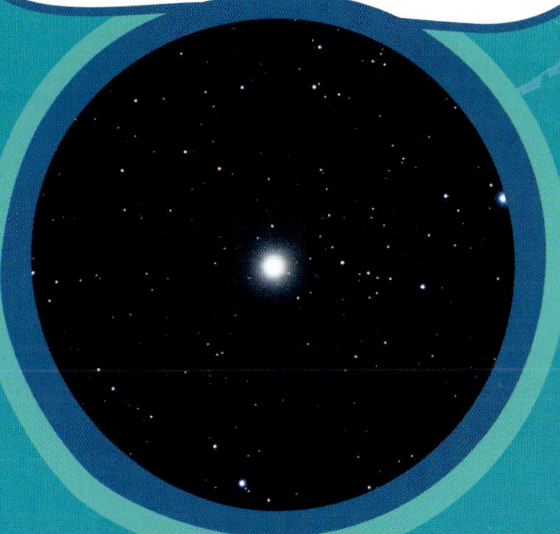

Asterisms

Some well-known star patterns aren't constellations but are asterisms. These are smaller than constellations but can be part of one, like the Plough, which is part of the constellation Ursa Major. Others, like the Summer Triangle, are made up of stars from more than one constellation.

Different seasons

From any place on Earth, we can only ever see half the sky at a time. In the UK, we can see about half of the 88 constellations on any given night, but the star patterns we see change throughout the year. As Earth orbits the Sun, our view of space shifts, meaning different constellations are visible in different seasons.

Light-years apart

Because we see the night sky as a flat starry canvas, it can seem like stars are close together. In reality, though, they are light-years apart! The Universe is three-dimensional, so some bright stars may be easier to see because they shine more strongly, while others look bright simply because they are closer to us.

Influential culture and history

Throughout history, people have used the stars to tell stories and connect them to heroes, gods and goddesses. But as we have learned more about stars, especially our own Sun, we have discovered the strong link between the Sun's activity and our lives on Earth.

DID YOU KNOW?

In 1543, it was the Polish astronomer Nicolaus Copernicus that proposed that the Sun was stationary at the centre of the Solar System, with Earth and the other planets orbiting around it.

Carrington Event

In 1859, Earth experienced its most powerful recorded solar storm, caused by a coronal mass ejection (CME). Known as the Carrington Event, it disrupted telegraph messaging systems and made auroras visible around the world. In North America, the aurora was so bright that some people could even read a newspaper by its light!

NEWS

Happy b-EARTH-day

We measure time by tracking Earth's movement around the Sun, and the time it takes to complete one full orbit is called a year. So, the next time you celebrate your birthday, remember – you've just completed another lap around the Sun!

Stories in the sky

48 of the 88 official constellations are named after Greek heroes, gods and goddesses, with others named after animals or objects. For centuries, people have looked up at the night sky, connecting stars to form pictures and creating stories about them. These tales often describe great adventures and, much like traditional fairy tales, carry important warnings or lessons.

Nancy Grace Roman

Having had a love for stars as a child, Nancy Grace Roman later became NASA's first Chief of Astronomy. She studied visible stars like the Sun and noticed that stars made of lighter elements tend to orbit near the centre of our galaxy, while those with heavier elements are usually found further out. Modern studies of how the Milky Way may have formed have been influenced by her valuable work.

Statue of Icarus in Cyprus

Icarus and the Sun

In Greek mythology, Icarus, the son of Daedalus, escaped imprisonment using wings his father made from feathers, thread and wax. Daedalus warned him not to fly too low, or the feathers would get wet, and not too high, or the Sun would scorch them. But Icarus soared too close to the Sun, and as the wax melted, his wings fell apart. He plunged into the sea, never to be seen again.

Constellation of Leo the Lion

Constellation of Taurus the Bull

Signs of the zodiac

In western astrology, 12 of the 88 constellations are known as the signs of the zodiac. They lie in a band across the sky that marks the plane of our Solar System. So in astronomy, these constellations can help locate things like the Sun, Moon and planets. In astrology, some people believe the star signs related to the zodiac constellations can reveal people's characters or predict the future.

Extraordinary missions

From Earth, we can feel the Sun's scorching heat and see its blinding light – so sending missions to study it is incredibly challenging! Designing spacecraft to survive the Sun's extreme conditions requires skill and ingenuity. But the valuable knowledge we can gain from studying it up-close makes these efforts worthwhile.

DID YOU KNOW?
The average distance between Earth and the Sun is 150 million kilometres.

Parker Solar Probe = 6.1 million km from the Sun

Parker Solar Probe

The Parker Solar Probe was launched in 2018 and will travel closer to the Sun than any other space probe. Eventually, it will be pulled apart when its thrusters run out of fuel.

Solar Orbiter = 77 million km from the Sun

Solar Orbiter

ESA's Solar Orbiter was launched in 2020 to help answer big questions about the Sun. It was the first satellite to capture close-up views of the Sun's polar regions.

SOHO

The joint NASA and ESA mission, SOHO, is the longest-running mission studying the Sun. It was designed to explore the Sun's structure and activity, and how it interacts with Earth. Alongside this, SOHO has discovered more comets than any other instrument in history – tracking them as they pass close to the Sun.

SDO

NASA's Solar Dynamics Observatory (SDO) has been orbiting Earth since 2010, helping us understand the Sun's influence on our planet. It studies solar activity and solar weather, examining how these affect the planet.

SDO = 36,000 km from Earth

SOHO = 1.5 million km from Earth

Aditya-L1 = 1.5 million km from Earth

Aditya-L1

Like the SOHO mission, the Indian space agency's (ISRO) first mission to study the Sun, Aditya-L1, is positioned at a special point between the Earth and the Sun called L1 Lagrange point. From here, the spacecraft observes the Sun's atmosphere, while any material the Sun ejects reaches it about an hour before reaching Earth. This makes it a useful solar watchdog!

NEXT STOP... GALAXIES

Galaxies

Go beyond the Milky Way to investigate other galaxies, and look out for some colourful and jaw-dropping sights – from sleepy stellar nurseries where stars are born, to chaotic collisions as galaxies merge together. Hope you've got your cameras ready!

The Milky Way

When we look up at the night sky, every star we see belongs to our own galaxy, the Milky Way. It's home to our Solar System, but also to countless other planetary systems scattered among the distant points of light. Although we've never travelled beyond our galaxy to see it from the outside, astronomers use scientific tools and techniques to study what it looks like and how it compares to others.

Galactic orbit

All the stars in our galaxy orbit around the centre of the Milky Way, just like planets circle the Sun. Our star, located about halfway out from the centre, takes 225 million years to complete one full orbit. The last time it finished a lap, dinosaurs were just beginning to appear on Earth!

Positioning of the Sun

Other side of the galaxy

Our galaxy is about 100,000 light-years across. If you stood on one side and your friend was on the other, a text message (travelling at the speed of light) would take 100,000 years to reach them – that's quite a wait!

Local Group

Like a galactic family, the Local Group is a collection of galaxies within about 5 million light-years of space around us. The Milky Way is one of the three largest galaxies in this group – the biggest is Andromeda, while the Triangulum galaxy is slightly smaller than ours. The rest of the 50 or so galaxies in the Local Group are much smaller dwarf galaxies.

Andromeda

Billions of stars

Because we're inside our galaxy, it's difficult to count all the stars. But astronomers estimate there are between 100 billion and 400 billion in the Milky Way – and the Sun is just one of them!

Dwarf galaxies

Astronomers have discovered about 50 dwarf galaxies swarming around our own. The two largest, containing just a few billion stars, are called the Large Magellanic Cloud and the Small Magellanic Cloud. From the Southern Hemisphere, they look like hazy clouds of stars. A stream of gas and stars connects them, which suggests they have interacted in the past.

DID YOU KNOW?

Our galaxy is thought to be around 13.6 billion years old, but it probably took the first few billion years of this to form most of its stars. When the Universe was young, galaxies like ours were producing more than a dozen stars every year. Today, the Milky Way creates only about one new star per year.

How old?!

Warped and wobbling

Although we imagine the Milky Way as a flat disc, it's actually slightly warped – curving upwards on one side and downwards on the other. This 'warp' slowly wobbles around the centre of our galaxy, a bit like a spinning top. Scientists think this happens because of the tilted cloud of dark matter surrounding our galaxy.

Spiral galaxy

The Milky Way is a spiral galaxy with a bar-like shape at its centre. At the heart of our galaxy is a supermassive black hole called Sagittarius A*. Most of the gas, dust and stars are contained within its flat spiral disc. However, the galaxy is also surrounded by a spherical halo that stretches about 1 million light-years from the centre.

Types of galaxies

Galaxies come in all sorts of shapes, sizes and colours, which makes them fascinating to observe. Sometimes, they can be tricky to identify because of the way they're positioned from our point of view – so astronomers have to do a bit of detective work. While spiral galaxies like the Milky Way are the most common, naming the more unusual ones based on what they look like can be entertaining!

Spiral galaxy

Spiral galaxies holding millions of stars just like the Milky way can be spotted in our night skies. They can be either normal spiral or barred spiral galaxies. In a normal spiral galaxy, the spiral starts from the central bulge and in a barred spiral the arms instead begin at the ends of the central bar that runs through the bulge.

NGC 1300

Abell S0740

Elliptical galaxy

Elliptical galaxies are just that – elliptical in shape, with a rather smooth and featureless appearance. They are thought to be home to more of the oldest stars in the Universe than any other type of galaxy.

Irregular galaxy

Neither elliptical nor spiral, irregular galaxies don't fit the norm. They can look quite strange and are thought to make up around 20% of all galaxies in the Universe. Good examples of these are the Large and Small Magellanic Clouds, which are found just outside our own galaxy.

NGC 2337

NGC 4866

Lenticular galaxy

Lenticular galaxies are a mix between spiral and elliptical galaxies. They have the same central bulge as a spiral galaxy but lack the spiral arms. Scientists think they may have evolved from old spiral galaxies that 'lost' their arms or formed from galaxies merging together.

Starburst galaxy

The stars in starburst galaxies form much faster than in most others. One example is M82, located 12 million light-years away in the constellation of Ursa Major. This galaxy is creating new stars at 10 times the rate of the Milky Way!

Dwarf galaxy

Dwarf galaxies contain only a few billion stars, while elliptical or spiral galaxies can have around 200 billion. So, it's easy to see why they're called dwarf galaxies! Despite their small size, astronomers think they can help us to understand how the Universe has changed over time.

Arp 142

Interacting galaxy

Interacting galaxies are ones that collide or influence each other in some way. A good example is the Penguin and Egg galaxies, known as Arp 142. Their interaction is thought to have begun around 50 million years ago – and they will continue to dance around each other for hundreds of millions of years before eventually merging into a single galaxy.

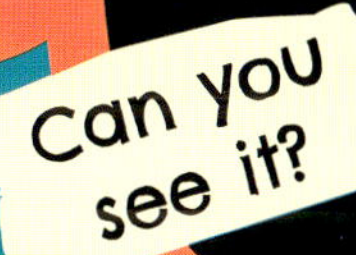

Hoag's Object

Ring galaxy

A ring galaxy is shaped like a ring and is usually made up of young, massive, bright blue stars. The most unusual example is Hoag's Object, which has a ring of these bright blue stars but also a central region of older, yellow stars.

Ultra-diffuse galaxy

NGC 1052-DF2

Ultra-diffuse galaxies, or dark galaxies, are much fainter than most other galaxies and have some unusual features. Some are jam-packed with dark matter, while others seem to have very little. They also contain dense groupings of old stars. These strange properties continue to puzzle scientists.

Active galaxies

Many galaxies are so far away that they can be difficult to observe. But active galaxies, which were once the brightest known objects in the Universe, allow us to peer back in time to the distant past. They can teach us how the Universe may have formed, what black holes are like and how high-energy radiation is created in space.

NGC 5728

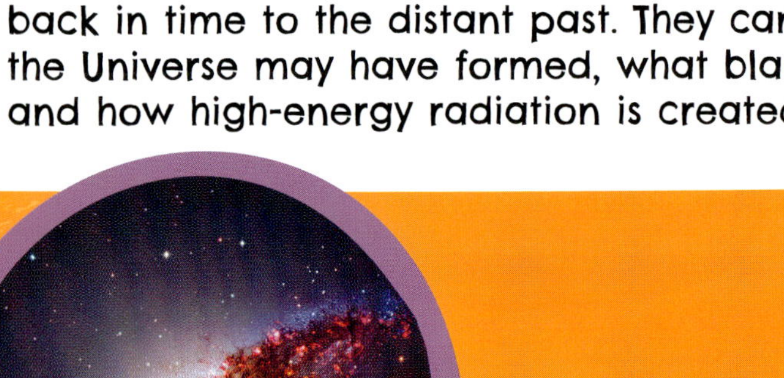

NGC 5128

Radio galaxies

Radio galaxies also contain an AGN, but they are different from some of the other galaxies we've looked at. They produce more radio waves than visible light waves, so astronomers find them by detecting radio signals with telescopes rather than with the light we see with our eyes.

Seyfert galaxies

Seyfert galaxies were first classified in 1943. These are a type of super bright spiral galaxy that contain an AGN. Scientists believe that studying them could help us learn more about how galaxies change over time.

What is an active galaxy?

An active galaxy is one which has a supermassive black hole at its centre that is feeding on the matter around it. This region at the centre of the galaxy which gives off huge amounts of energy is called an Active Galactic Nucleus (AGN), and it is extremely bright, making active galaxies easier to observe even at a distance!

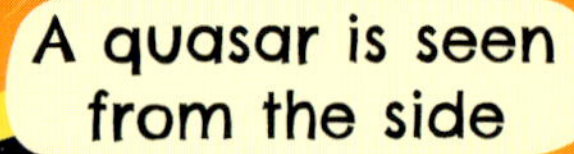

A quasar is seen from the side

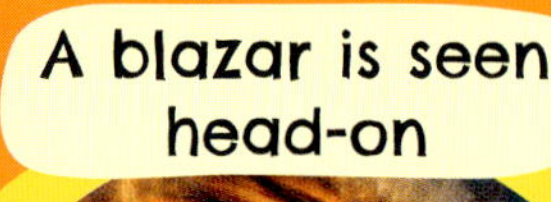

A blazar is seen head-on

Quasars

Quasars are a type of AGN that are found in young galaxies billions of light-years away, and can shine more than 25 trillion times brighter than the Sun! So far, more than 900,000 quasars have been discovered.

VS.

Blazars

The main difference between a blazar and a quasar is the angle from which we see it. Both are AGN with supermassive black holes and powerful jets of radiation streaming from them. However, a blazar's jet is directly pointed towards Earth, making it look much brighter.

The Hamburger Galaxy

Centaurus A is a radio galaxy in the constellation Centaurus that contains an AGN. It's the fifth brightest galaxy in the sky but can only be seen from the Southern Hemisphere. At about 11 million light-years away, it's the closest active galaxy to Earth. Because of its appearance it has earned the nickname 'the Hamburger Galaxy'.

Exciting discovery

In 1908, astronomers Edward A. Fath and Vesto Slipher saw bright light coming from what they thought was a spiral nebula – providing the first evidence for active galaxies. However, it wasn't until 1943, when Carl Keenan Seyfert found more galaxies with the same unusual features, that the idea of active galaxies really took shape.

High energy

Active galaxies can give off thousands of times more energy than normal galaxies, but much of it is more than visible light from stars. Huge amounts of X-rays, powerful jets of radio waves and infrared radiation are emitted from them.

Star clusters

The gravitational pull of a galaxy holds its stars together, but within it, there are pockets of stars called clusters. Like cities filled with people, star clusters are groups of stars gathered close together that formed around the same time. These 'laboratories in the sky' help astronomers to study how stars change over time.

The Sun's siblings

Stars are born in groups from a giant cloud of gas and dust. But if that's the case, where are the Sun's siblings? Although they may have formed together, gravitational tugs between the stars and from those outside the cluster have, over time, scattered them across the Milky Way.

Neighbours

It's estimated that stars in the Milky Way are about five light-years apart – the distance between the Sun and our next nearest star is just under this amount. But in the spherical halo around our galaxy, we find clusters of stars where the distance between the members is just one light-year apart!

Open cluster

An open cluster is a group of a few hundred to a few thousand stars. Gravity pulls them together but because there aren't many stars, this force is weak – resulting in an irregular shape. The Pleiades is a good example of an open cluster of stars.

Baby stars

In the Pleiades, also known as the Seven Sisters, six of the stars are easy to see with the naked eye, lying within the constellation of Taurus. They are hot, bright blue stars and only about 100 million years old – young for stars! The Pleiades is around 440 light-years away from Earth.

Pleiades, open cluster

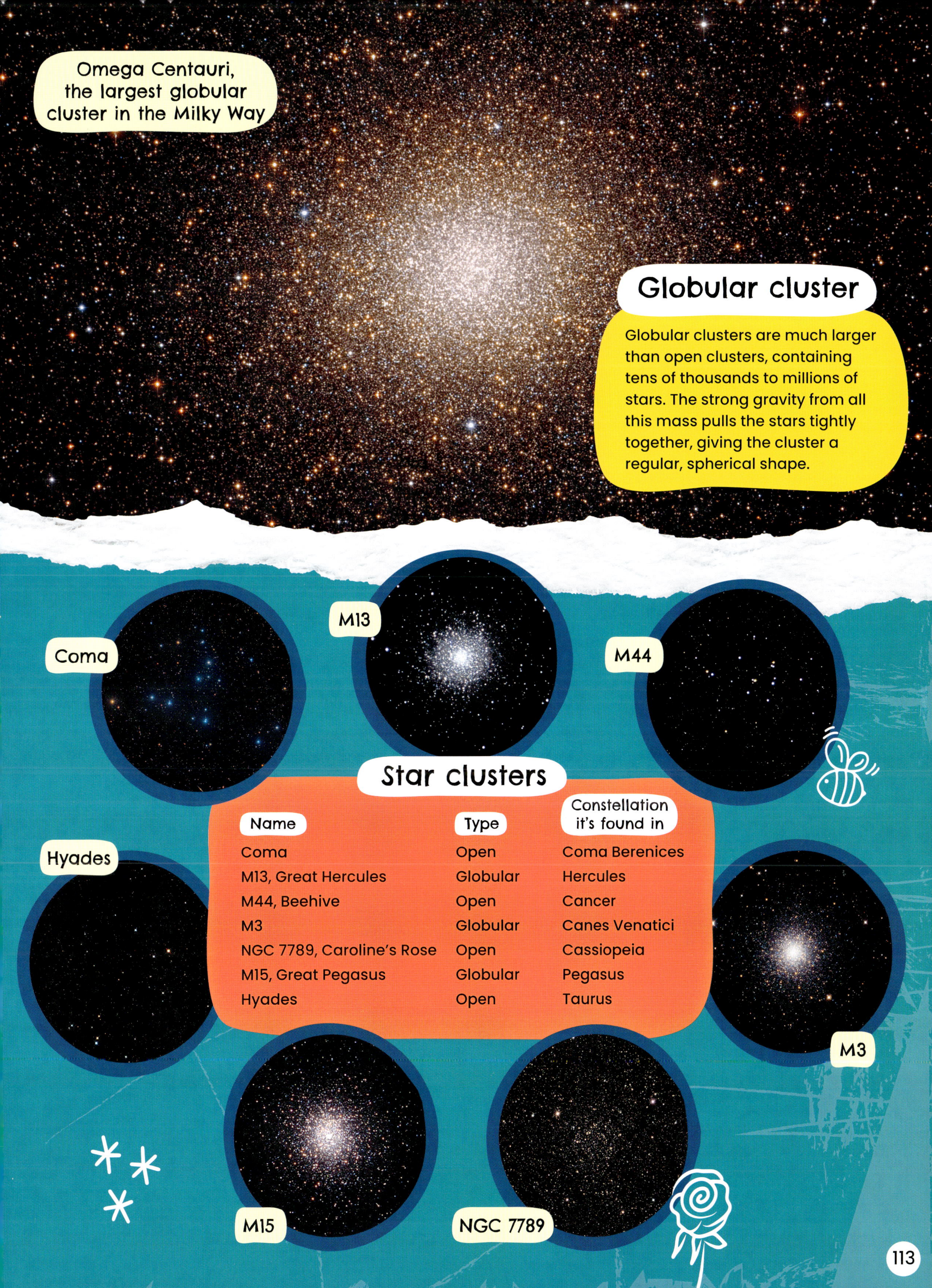

Globular cluster

Globular clusters are much larger than open clusters, containing tens of thousands to millions of stars. The strong gravity from all this mass pulls the stars tightly together, giving the cluster a regular, spherical shape.

Star clusters

Name	Type	Constellation it's found in
Coma	Open	Coma Berenices
M13, Great Hercules	Globular	Hercules
M44, Beehive	Open	Cancer
M3	Globular	Canes Venatici
NGC 7789, Caroline's Rose	Open	Cassiopeia
M15, Great Pegasus	Globular	Pegasus
Hyades	Open	Taurus

Astronomical wonders

Galaxies are some of the largest structures in the Universe and so galactic events often happen over very large timescales. Astronomers study the present-day Universe to piece together cosmic events, from the birth of galaxies to their eventual death.

Out of gas!

Quenching

When a galaxy stops forming stars, it's called 'quenching', and the galaxy is said to be 'quiescent'. Scientists think this happens for a few reasons – a galaxy could run out of gas needed to make new stars, or a supermassive black hole at its centre might interfere with star formation. The Milky Way is thought to have slowed its star formation to almost a stop around eight billion years ago.

Galaxies collide

Scientists believe that the Andromeda Galaxy, with around a trillion stars, and the Milky Way, with about 300 billion, will one day collide as gravity pulls them together. This might sound scary, but when it happens in about 4.5 billion years, it's very unlikely that any stars or planets will crash into each other because of the vast distances between them. However, some stars may be flung out of the newly formed galaxy.

NGC 2444

NGC 2445

An interacting galaxy duo called Arp 143

S1
S3
S2

Three red monsters, captured by the James Webb Space Telescope

Red Monsters

Some massive galaxies in the early Universe appear red in colour because of the huge amounts of dust inside them. These 'Red Monsters' discovered by the James Webb Space Telescope were creating stars much faster than expected. They were already fully formed within the first billion years of the Universe – challenging the idea that galaxies grow slowly over time.

R.I.P

What came first?

Did stars form first and then merge into galaxies, or did galaxies take shape as the first stars developed? Many scientists now think that the first structures to form were mini-haloes, the smallest structures in the early Universe made of a mysterious and invisible substance called dark matter. These mini-haloes pulled in surrounding gas with their gravity, and from that, the first stars were able to form. Over time, by attracting and holding on to more matter, larger objects like galaxies were able to take shape.

Zombie galaxies

When a galaxy eventually runs out of gas, it can no longer make new stars. As its stars grow old and die, so too does the galaxy. Sometimes, interactions with other galaxies strip away the gas needed to form stars, bringing an early end. Some galaxies contain mostly dying stars with very little star formation – they are more or less dead and are known as 'zombie galaxies'.

On the move

In 1929, Edwin Hubble noticed that all galaxies appear to be moving away from Earth. His discovery was due to something called 'redshift'. As a galaxy moves away, the light it gives out shifts towards the red end of the colour spectrum – and this redshift is how we know the Universe is still expanding.

Illustration of zombie galaxy MACS2129-1

Influential culture and history

Before light pollution dulled the night sky, the glowing band of the Milky Way was easy to see – and in remote, dark places, it still is. But it's only in the last century that real progress has been made in understanding the Milky Way and other galaxies. Throughout history, it has inspired myths and legends, as well as sparked our imagination about what lies beyond – especially in science fiction.

DID YOU KNOW?
In Greek myths, the Milky Way was said to be milk spilled across the heavens by the goddess Hera. Different cultures have their own legends – the Egyptians saw the starry sky as the goddess Nut who swallowed the Sun at night, while in China, it's called the 'Silver River'.

Hubble Deep Field

In 1996, the Hubble Space Telescope focused on a tiny patch of sky – about the size of a grain of rice held at arm's length. Though it seemed empty at first, Hubble collected the faint light of distant galaxies in a series of images taken over 10 days. Combining all the data, astronomers created the final image, known as the iconic Hubble Deep Field. It showed around 3,000 galaxies and, at the time, it was the deepest view of the Universe ever taken.

Fuzzy nebulae

For many centuries, galaxies visible to the naked eye (like Andromeda) were known as 'fuzzy nebulae' and were thought to be inside the Milky Way. In 1924, astronomer Edwin Hubble used a special type of pulsing star called a 'Cepheid variable' to measure the distance to Andromeda. He discovered it was much greater than the size of the Milky Way – proving it was a galaxy beyond our own.

Back in time

The light from distant stars and galaxies we see in the night sky can take millions of years to reach us. So when we see stars in space, it's like looking back in time.

The Messier Catalogue

In the seventeenth century, astronomer Charles Messier observed more than 100 distant objects and recorded them in numerical order in his catalogue. Although he was searching for comets, he also found several fuzzy objects – which we now know to be galaxies and nebulae.

Messier objects

Name	Type	Constellation it's found in
M13, Great Hercules	Globular cluster	Hercules
M14	Globular cluster	Ophiuchus
M15, Great Pegasus	Globular cluster	Pegasus
M16, Eagle Nebula	Nebula + open cluster	Serpens
M17, Omega Nebula	Nebula	Sagittarius

DID YOU KNOW?

All Messier objects start with the letter M. Similarly in other catalogues – like the New General Catalogue of nebulae, galaxies and star clusters – all the objects begin with NGC.

Hyperspace

Travelling vast distances across our galaxy isn't a reality for us – but in science fiction, anything is possible! In *Star Wars*™, starships enter a dimension called hyperspace. This allows them to travel faster than the speed of light, making galactic travel achievable.

Extraordinary missions

Travelling through our Solar System is challenging enough, so sending missions beyond our galaxy is out of the question for now. Instead, scientists and engineers use creative methods to study incredibly distant objects without ever getting close to them. Like detectives at a crime scene, they carefully piece together clues to unravel galactic mysteries.

Gaia

Mapping the Milky Way

From observing billions of stars, data from the Gaia mission is being used to create a 3D map of the Milky Way. By scanning the sky as it orbited the Sun from its position 1.5 million kilometres from Earth, it precisely tracked the positions of stars over time. This mission is helping us uncover the origins and evolution of our galaxy.

James Webb Space Telescope

JWST heading into space in a rocket

JWST

The James Webb Space Telescope (JWST) launched on 25 December 2021 and was designed to help us understand distant objects in our Universe by peering further back in time than ever before. Its main mirror is about 6.5 metres wide – so large that it had to be folded to fit inside the rocket before launch.

Galaxies missions (launch dates)

Hubble (orbiter) 24 Apr 1990

Two Micron All Sky Survey (2MASS) (based on Earth) 7 Jun 1997

Hubble

The Hubble Space Telescope was launched in April 1990. Shortly after, scientists noticed that the images it sent back were blurry due to a tiny flaw in its mirror – an error smaller than the width of a human hair. In 1993, a mission with seven astronauts was sent to fix the problem – a bit like putting on a pair of glasses to improve vision!

Hubble launch, 24 April 1990

Countless galaxies

Thanks to the Hubble Space Telescope, scientists have discovered that there are more than two trillion galaxies in the known Universe – 10 times more than previously thought! Each galaxy contains billions of stars. In fact, there are believed to be more stars in space than grains of sand on all the beaches on Earth.

Hubble Space Telescope

Sloan Digital Sky Survey

The Sloan Digital Sky Survey began in 2000 and is still running today. It uses a 2.5-metre-wide optical telescope at Apache Point Observatory in New Mexico to create the most detailed 3D map of the Universe. This project has revealed details about the features, structure and distribution of millions of galaxies across the cosmos.

Apache Point Observatory

Galaxy Evolution Explorer (orbiter) 28 Apr 2003

Sloan Digital Sky Survey (based on Earth) 27 Oct 2003

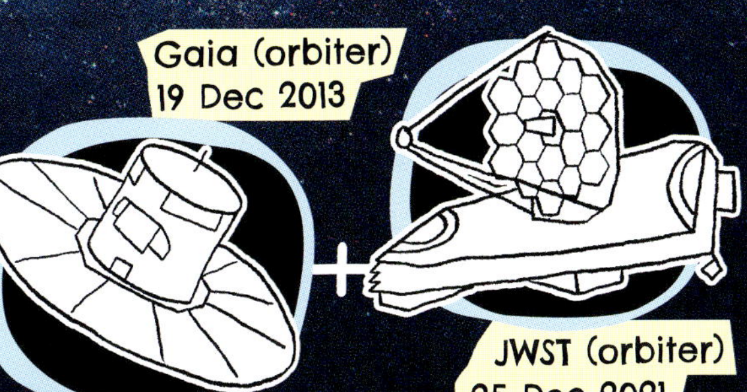

Gaia (orbiter) 19 Dec 2013

JWST (orbiter) 25 Dec 2021

NEXT STOP... INVISIBLE SPACE

Invisible
Space

The final destination on the tour brings together the invisible and intriguing treasures of space. From explosive beginnings to the probable ends to the Universe, there's still so much for us to explore and uncover. What cosmic mysteries might you help solve in the future?

The Big Bang

Most scientists believe that the Universe began with the Big Bang. Observations show that the Universe appears to be expanding, so it's thought to have begun as a tiny, hot and dense point containing all the energy that makes up everything we see today. This point sprang into existence 13.8 billion years ago, bringing time, space and matter into being.

The first particles

The very early Universe was incredibly hot and dense. Within the first second after the Big Bang, some of the very first particles began to form. First came tiny particles called neutrinos, quarks and electrons. Then, as the Universe expanded and cooled, the quarks combined to form the first protons and neutrons.

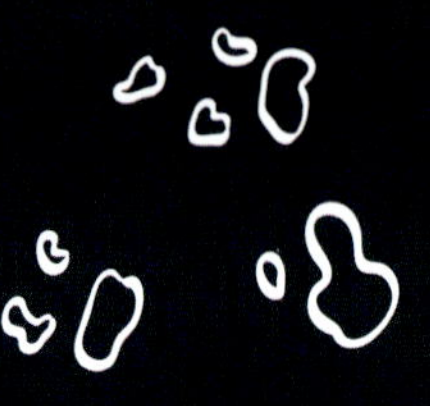

The Big Bang

Rapid expansion

In the fraction of a second after the Big Bang, the Universe expanded faster than the speed of light. This period is known as 'inflation'. Over time, the denser parts of the early Universe went on to become huge galaxy clusters and the low-density parts became voids – the huge empty regions in space between the clusters.

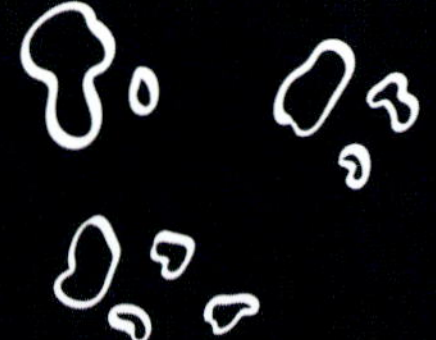

Time since the Big Bang →

10-32 seconds	1 microsecond	3 minutes	380,000 years
Initial expansion	First particles	First nuclei	First atoms

Atomic nucleus

About three minutes after the Big Bang, as the Universe cooled further, protons and neutrons began to join to form nuclei – the central part of an atom. This process, called 'nucleosynthesis', continued for around 20 minutes.

Earliest atoms

Around 380,000 years later, the Universe had cooled enough for the first atoms to form from atomic nuclei and electrons coming together. Before this, it was still too hot, and the energetic soup of cosmic particles couldn't stay together. As a result, mostly hydrogen, some helium, and tiny amounts of lithium and beryllium filled the Universe.

Stars and galaxies

A few hundred million years after the Big Bang, the first stars and galaxies began to form. Gas and dust in the denser regions were pulled closer together by gravity, causing the Universe to light up. The most intense period of star and galaxy formation occurred a few billion years after the Big Bang.

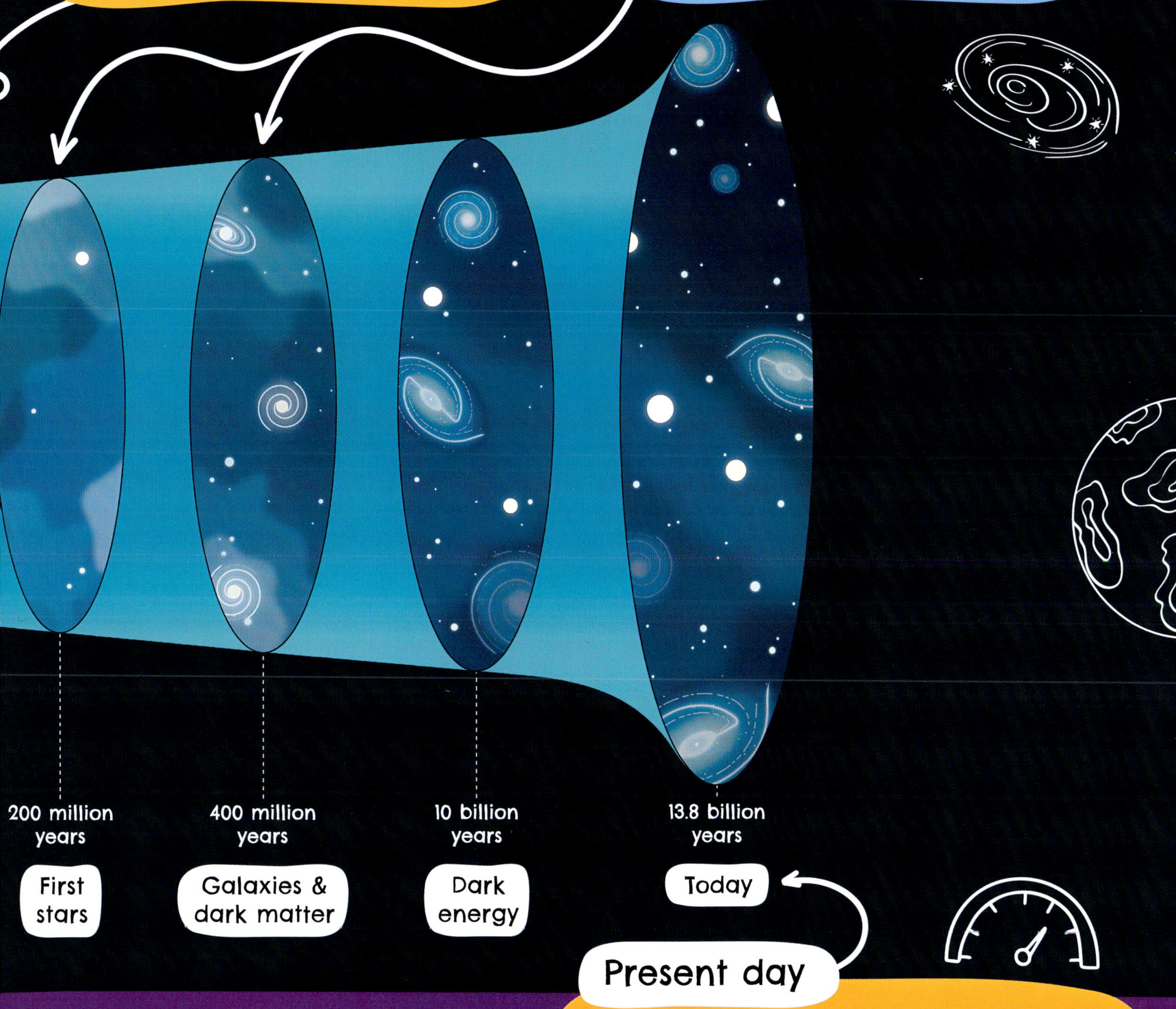

Present day

Today, the formation of stars and galaxies has slowed, but the Universe continues to expand – and it's speeding up due to the influence of dark energy (see page 129). This means the Universe is expanding faster now than it did yesterday and will expand even faster tomorrow!

Black holes

Black holes have fascinated scientists for years. They were first discovered in 1964, although astronomers thought they existed as far back as the eighteenth century. These objects are so dense, with gravity so strong that even light cannot escape their pull. Their effects can be seen throughout the Universe – but don't worry, they are too far away to cause us any harm!

Spaghettification

When objects get too close to a black hole, 'spaghettification' happens. The distance at which this occurs depends on the size of the black hole and its gravitational pull. Once an object is too close, it can't escape and gets stretched out and pulled apart. Because gravity pulls at different strengths across the object, over time it would stretch so much that it would look like a piece of spaghetti!

Event horizon

A black hole's 'event horizon' is the boundary around it where gravity is so strong that even light cannot escape. Once something crosses this boundary, it can never get out. The size of the event horizon depends on the black hole's mass and can range from six miles across to larger than the entire Solar System.

Accretion disk

An accretion disk is a flat disk surrounding and orbiting a black hole. It is made up of material such as gas and dust pulled in by gravity.

The first ever image of a black hole

M87, supermassive black hole

Caught on camera

Before 2019, black holes could only be identified by their effects on the space around them. That changed when the Event Horizon Telescope captured the first-ever image of a black hole at the centre of the M87 galaxy. The photo shows a glowing ring of light surrounding a dark circle – the black hole.

DID YOU KNOW?
Time near a black hole slows down as space and time warps. This is known as 'time dilation'.

Types of black holes

Supermassive

A supermassive black hole (SMBH) is the biggest kind of black hole. It can be billions of times the mass of the Sun and is found in the middle of galaxies like the Milky Way. The supermassive black hole at the centre of our galaxy is around 4 million times the mass of our Sun.

DID YOU KNOW?
The first object to be identified as a black hole was Cygnus X-1 in 1971.

Stellar

Stellar black holes are smaller than supermassive black holes. These form when a massive star collapses and they are typically between five to ten times the mass of our Sun, though some can be larger. The nearest one to us is Gaia BH1 – it's over 1,500 light-years away and is ten times the mass of our Sun.

Primordial

Although there's no definite proof, scientists think there could be tiny black holes, called primordial black holes. These are believed to have formed in the first second after the birth of the Universe.

Gravitational waves

Exploring space is already difficult because everything is so far away, but another challenge is that much of the Universe is invisible to us. Unseen gravitational waves, which ripple through space, offer a new way to study the cosmos. Although first predicted by Einstein more than 100 years ago, it was thought that gravitational waves would only ever be detected from space, but with modern technology, it's possible from right here on Earth.

What causes gravitational waves?

Gravitational waves can be like ripples in a pond that fade away. They are caused when massive objects rapidly speed up in space – such as when stars explode in supernovae, neutron stars spin, black holes form, or when these objects collide or orbit each other.

90°

LIGO

LIGO (Laser Interferometer Gravitational-Wave Observatory) is a giant experiment that helps scientists detect gravitational waves in space. Two enormous arms are set at a 90-degree angle to each other. A laser beam is split in two, with each part travelling down one of the arms and reflecting off mirrors at the end. If a gravitational wave passes through, it changes how the light waves move, and scientists can detect this tiny difference.

Detectors around the world

The LIGO experiment is based in the USA, but there are other gravitational wave detectors too. VIRGO is located in Italy and KAGRA is in Japan. These observatories often work together to identify where any detected gravitational waves came from.

One of LIGO's long arms in Livingston, Louisiana, USA

Gravitational wave

Black holes

Grid = fabric of space time

Black hole collision

Gravitational waves were first detected in 2015 by the LIGO and VIRGO experiments. They came from two black holes colliding into each other 1.3 billion years ago! By the time these ripples reached Earth, they were much fainter than their violent origins.

Albert Einstein

DID YOU KNOW?

Gravitational waves travel at the speed of light, but we can't see them through telescopes like we do with different types of light. Instead, scientists need incredibly sensitive instruments like interferometers to detect them.

The fabric of space-time

You might have heard the phrase 'the fabric of space-time' – but what does it mean? Albert Einstein first proposed this idea in his theory of general relativity. It explains how gravity distorts and curves space. The more massive an object is, the more it distorts space – and the larger the ripple or gravitational wave.

The dark universe

When we look up at the night sky, space looks dark – but it really is dark! That's because most of it is made of 'stuff' we can't see. Dark matter is invisible material that holds things together with its gravity, while dark energy is a mysterious force pushing the Universe apart. Scientists have found evidence that both exist, but they are still trying to work out exactly what they are.

Dark matter

Swiss astronomer Fritz Zwicky first put forward the idea of dark matter in 1933. While studying a group of galaxies called the Coma Cluster, he noticed there wasn't enough gravity from visible objects to keep the fast-moving galaxies from being flung out of the cluster – just like you would be flung off a roundabout that was spinning fast. This led him to believe there must be some unseen matter holding them together. The only way to detect dark matter is to observe its effects on the space around it, because it cannot be seen itself.

DID YOU KNOW?
Fritz Zwicky described the dark matter that he identified as 'dunkie materie'.

The Coma Cluster

Galaxy glue

In the 1970s, the idea of dark matter became more widely accepted after astronomer Vera Rubin studied how stars rotate in galaxies. We'd expect that those near the edges would move slower – like how the most distant planet, Neptune, orbits the Sun slower than the innermost planet, Mercury. But she discovered that stars at the edges of a galaxy were instead moving just as fast as those near the centre. Like invisible glue, the gravity of dark matter must be holding the galaxy together.

Vera Rubin at Kitt Peak National Observatory, USA, in 1963

What is the Universe made of?

All the visible matter, light and energy that we can detect makes up only five per cent of the Universe. That means 95 per cent is still a huge unknown! Dark matter, which outweighs visible matter nearly six times, makes up about 27 per cent, while the biggest chunk (around 68 per cent) is the bit we know the least about – dark energy.

DID YOU KNOW?

After the initial expansion of the Big Bang, the pull of gravity began to slow down the expansion of the Universe. But after nine billion years, the expansion began to speed up, driven by dark energy.

Dark energy

Following the Big Bang and the initial expansion of the Universe, scientists would expect the gravity of objects to pull on each other and slow this expansion down. But instead, observations have shown the Universe is expanding at a faster rate. The current explanation proposed in 1998 is an anti-gravity force, which we call dark energy, pushing the Universe apart.

Astronomical wonders

The Universe is an amazing place, full of wonders and mysteries. Despite all that we have discovered, there is still so much to explore and many questions yet to be answered. Some of the biggest puzzles for scientists include what was the very early Universe like, what is dark matter and dark energy, how did galaxies and stars evolve, and what will happen when the Universe comes to an end?

DID YOU KNOW?

Because the amount and effects of dark matter and dark energy are still not very well understood, our predictions about the end of the Universe could completely change in the future.

Higgs boson

In 2012, scientists in Switzerland discovered the Higgs boson – sometimes called the Higgs particle – using the Large Hadron Collider (LHC). This particle is believed to give everything mass, including stars and planets.

Dark matter detective

The LHC is a ring-shaped tunnel that smashes particles together at close to the speed of light. By doing so, it can create conditions similar to the early Universe where dark matter particles might be produced. Scientists hope to be able to study interactions with other particles that we can detect, to give us clues about what dark matter really is.

Large Hadron Collider at CERN in Switzerland

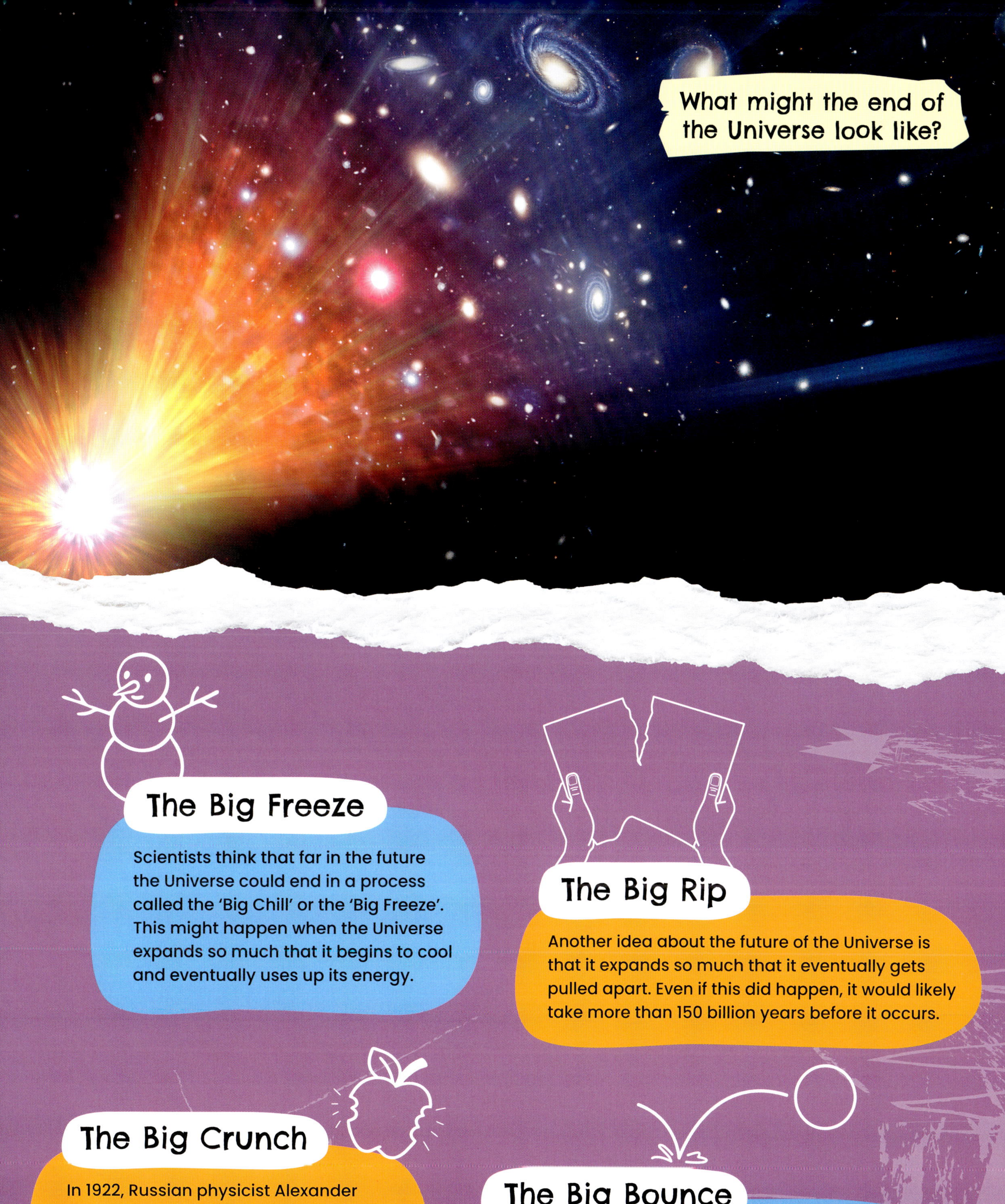

The Big Freeze

Scientists think that far in the future the Universe could end in a process called the 'Big Chill' or the 'Big Freeze'. This might happen when the Universe expands so much that it begins to cool and eventually uses up its energy.

The Big Rip

Another idea about the future of the Universe is that it expands so much that it eventually gets pulled apart. Even if this did happen, it would likely take more than 150 billion years before it occurs.

The Big Crunch

In 1922, Russian physicist Alexander Friedmann proposed that the Universe might eventually stop expanding and start to shrink. This could cause it to collapse in on itself, like a giant black hole, pulling everything with it.

The Big Bounce

Another idea is that the Universe might not end but instead go through cycles of expansion and contraction. We may currently be going through an expansion phase and in the future, the Universe could contract and then 'bounce' back into expanding again.

Influential culture and history

For a long time, the understanding of our Universe was limited to our Solar System and galaxy. But in the twentieth century, scientists made great progress in defining the laws of physics that explain what we see in nature. These new ideas gave us a much bigger picture of the cosmos – how it looks, what it's made of and how it behaves.

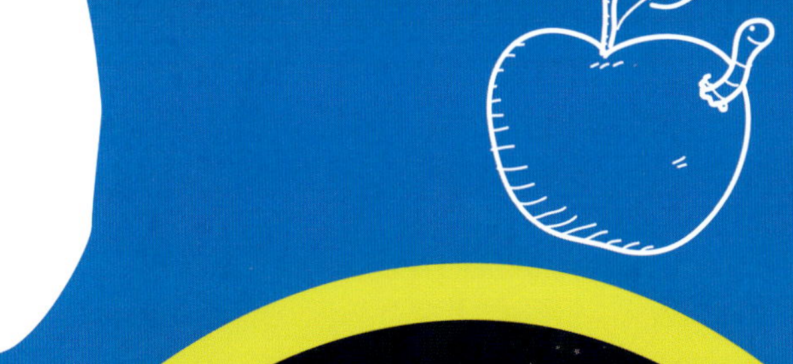

Wormholes

Like secret tunnels, wormholes are imagined portholes that link two points in space-time. Although none have ever been discovered, they are popular in sci-fi films like *Interstellar* and *Thor*, where they let characters travel across the galaxy or even act as time machines!

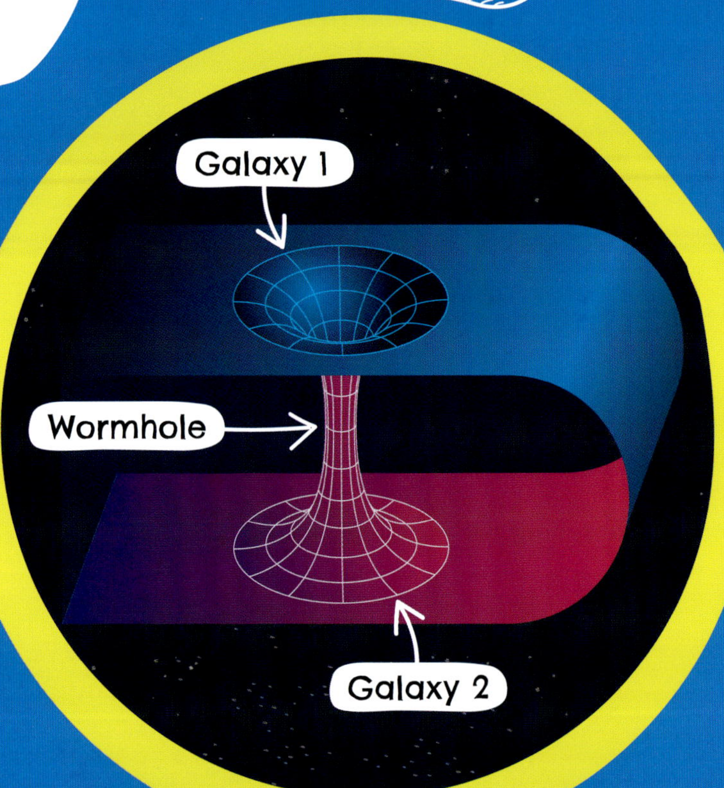

2012

In the film *2012*, the destruction of the Earth's crust is blamed on dangerous 'mutated' neutrinos from the Sun. In reality, the Sun constantly sends out neutrinos, which are tiny particles that are completely harmless. In fact, around 100 trillion neutrinos pass through our bodies every second without us even noticing!

Hafele-Keating experiment

In 1971, two scientists, Hafele and Keating, carried out an experiment by flying very precise clocks, called atomic clocks, around the world on aeroplanes and comparing them to clocks left on the ground. The flying clocks ran slightly slower because of their higher speed – meaning that by travelling faster, you actually age more slowly! This is known as time dilation.

$E = mc^2$

Single theory

In 1900, physicist Max Planck introduced ideas that led to the development of quantum mechanics – a branch of science that explains how tiny particles behave. In 1915, Einstein presented his theory of general relativity, which describes gravity and the large-scale Universe. Both theories work well on their own, but when used together to study things like black holes or the extreme conditions of the early Universe, they don't fully agree. Scientists hope to find a single theory that works for both.

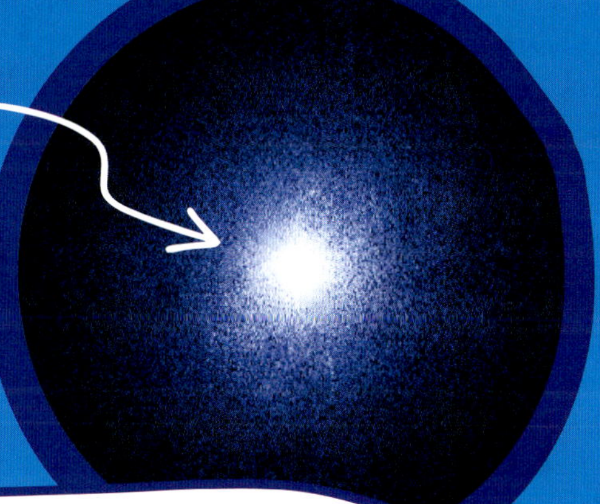

Cygnus X-1

DID YOU KNOW?

Einstein's theory of general relativity predicted the existence of black holes back in 1915. That's 56 years before the black hole Cygnus X-1 was identified, in 1971.

Einstein at his chalkboard

Static universe

Einstein proposed in 1917 that the Universe was static (not moving or changing). He completely rejected the idea of an expanding Universe until 1931.

Extraordinary missions

From the tiniest particles to the vastness of space, exploring the Universe has led to some engineering masterpieces. Scientists have invented telescopes with 'eyes' that can capture the light of the most distant objects and built experiments sensitive enough to detect tiny, split-second changes. These incredible projects have transformed our knowledge of space.

Hubble

The Hubble Space Telescope has transformed how we see the Universe. It has helped map the cosmos, showing where dark matter can be found. It has also discovered new moons, deepened our understanding of galaxy formation, identified exoplanets and much more.

Euclid

The ESA Euclid mission is named after an ancient Greek mathematician. It was designed to investigate what dark matter and dark energy are and how the Universe has expanded over time. Euclid will map billions of galaxies, capturing their light – which has taken up to ten billion years to reach us!

Pillars of Creation

James Webb Space Telescope

With its large mirror, the James Webb Space Telescope (JWST) is one of the most powerful and complex telescopes ever built. It uses infrared instruments to see the Universe in new ways, looking through dust and gas clouds to see stars hidden within. This helps scientists observe stars being born in regions like the Pillars of Creation and even study the atmospheres of exoplanets.

Telescope/observatory missions (launch dates)

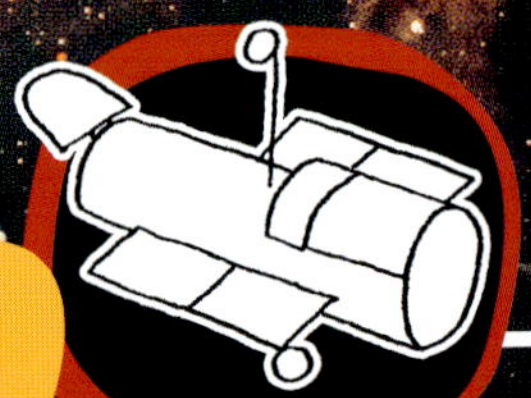

Hubble (orbiter) 24 Apr 1990

LIGO (based on Earth) 23 Aug 2002

Large Hadron Collider

The Large Hadron Collider (LHC) is the world's largest particle physics laboratory. This tunnel, with a circumference of 27 kilometres, is buried about 100 metres underground at the France-Switzerland border. Since it began operating in 2008, it has been smashing particles smaller than atoms together at nearly the speed of light. Scientists study these collisions to learn more about how the Universe works.

DID YOU KNOW?

The particles in the Large Hadron Collider are accelerated to 99.999999% the speed of light. Due to Einstein's theory of relativity, even though they are racing around a 27-kilometre ring, to the particles, it only seems like four metres!

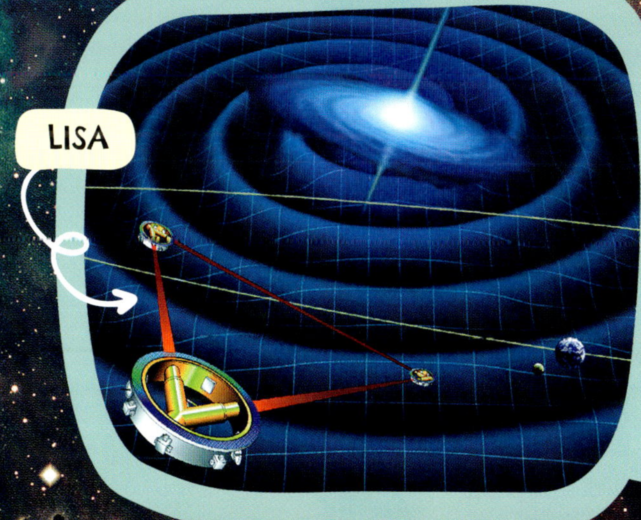

Gravitational wave detectors

LISA (Laser Interferometer Space Antenna) is planned to launch in 2035. It will be the first space-based observatory designed to study gravitational waves from merging black holes. On Earth, scientists have already used LIGO (Laser Interferometer Gravitational-Wave Observatory) to detect these waves.

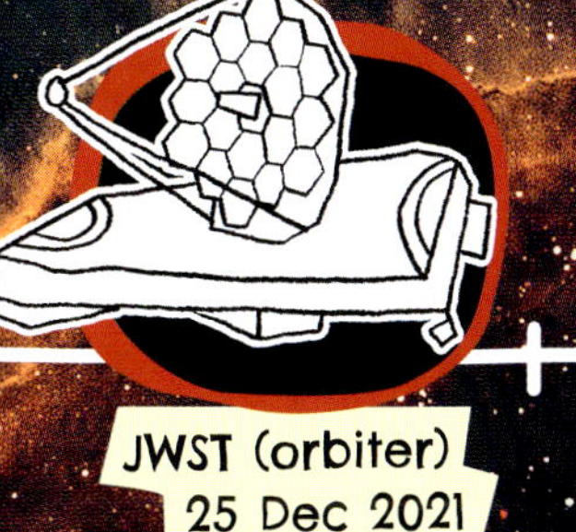

JWST (orbiter) 25 Dec 2021

Euclid (orbiter) 1 Jul 2023

XPoSat (orbiter) 1 Jan 2024

SPHEREx (orbiter) 11 Mar 2025

LISA (orbiter) 2035

Search for life

Using what we know about life on Earth, scientists have designed missions to search for planets beyond our Solar System. They've also tried to communicate with possible extraterrestrial life and work out the chances of finding it. Even though Earth is full of life, we haven't found anything out there – yet!

Kepler

NASA's first planet-hunting mission, the Kepler space telescope, was designed to look at a small portion of the sky for Earth-like planets orbiting other stars in the Milky Way. During its nine years in space, it found over 3,000 exoplanets. One of its biggest discoveries was the Kepler-90 system – the only known star system outside our own to have eight planets.

Kepler Space Telescope

Large Telescopes

The Very Large Telescope (VLT) in Chile is one of the world's most powerful telescopes. A new, even larger telescope, called the Extremely Large Telescope (ELT), is due to be completed in 2029. Its giant mirrors will allow it to see incredibly faint stars – some four billion times dimmer than what we can see with the naked eye! This will help astronomers peer back in time to study the Universe's history.

The VLT complex in the Atacama Desert, Chile

Search for life missions (launch dates)

Jodrell Bank Observatory (Lovell Telescope) (based on Earth) 2 Aug 1957

Arecibo (interstellar radio message) (based on Earth) 16 Nov 1974

VLT (based on Earth) 25 May 1998

TESS

Using the transit method – watching a star's light dim as a planet passes in front of it – NASA's Transiting Exoplanet Survey Satellite (TESS) mission spent two years searching for exoplanets around the brightest stars near Earth. These planets can then be studied in more detail by powerful telescopes, like the James Webb Space Telescope.

TESS

SETI

Search for Extraterrestrial Intelligence (SETI) is set up to look for signs of intelligent life beyond Earth. The SETI Breakthrough Listen programme has used a selection of telescopes to survey one million of the closest stars, collecting hundreds of hours of data. Launched in 2015, this ten-year project is searching for any signs of life or communication.

DID YOU KNOW?

In 1961, American astronomer Frank Drake proposed an equation to estimate how many alien civilisations in our galaxy might be able to communicate with us. However, some parts of the equation still have unknown values, so scientists can't solve it yet!

Jodrell Bank Observatory

The UK's largest radio telescope, the Lovell Telescope, can be found at Jodrell Bank, near Macclesfield. The telescope has played an important role in identifying quasars, meteorites and pulsars, among other things. It has also been used to look for SETI observations.

Arecibo Message

At just over 300 metres wide (about the size of three football pitches), the Arecibo Observatory was the world's second-largest single-dish radio telescope. Before its sudden collapse in late 2020, it made several important discoveries. In 1974, it was even used to send a message towards the globular cluster M13 in an attempt to contact extraterrestrial life.

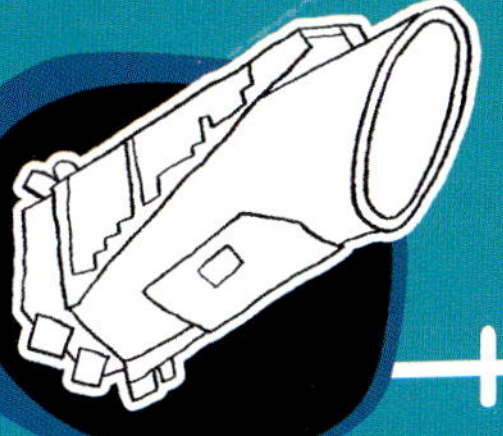

Kepler (K2) (orbiter) 6 Mar 2009

Sentinel (orbiter) 3 Apr 2014-present

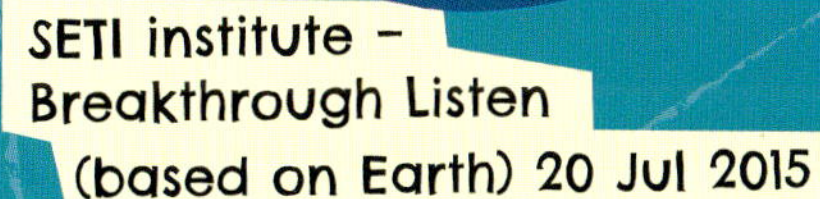

SETI institute – Breakthrough Listen (based on Earth) 20 Jul 2015

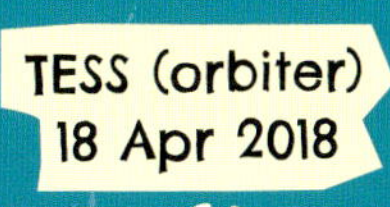

TESS (orbiter) 18 Apr 2018

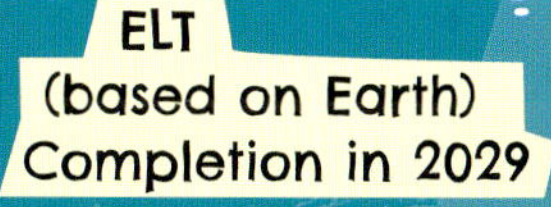

ELT (based on Earth) Completion in 2029

Mysteries of space

Although we've discovered a lot about the Universe, many things are still a great mystery. It's not surprising that the biggest questions are often about the changing Universe and the possibility of life beyond Earth. After all, the answers to these questions could reveal our origin story, the nature of reality and whether we're really alone in the cosmos.

What happened before the Big Bang?

Scientists aren't sure what happened before the Big Bang or what caused the rapid expansion that followed. Some think the energy needed to make the Universe expand was simply part of the fabric of space-time. Others believe the Universe may have shrunk into a tiny point, called a 'singularity', before bouncing back to create the Big Bang – and that universes may have been coming in and out of existence in cycles.

What is the Universe made of?

Our best estimates tell us that the Universe is made of a little visible matter, more dark matter and a large amount of dark energy. Scientists think dark matter and dark energy have played a big role in the formation and evolution of our Universe, and will likely determine its end too. But we still don't know what dark matter and dark energy are, even though they make up 95 per cent of our Universe.

Hubble Deep Field

Fact or science fiction?

Will we ever find life beyond Earth?

The Universe is huge, and there's still so much to explore and discover. New scientific methods and missions are helping us continue the search, but the truth is, we just don't know if we'll ever find life out there!

Are UFOs real?

Over the years, there have been many sightings of UFOs (which stands for Unidentified Flying Objects). While a few remain unexplained, most can be explained by natural events, hoaxes or human technology. Sometimes, aircraft are mistaken for UFOs, and some pranksters have used camera parts and lamp covers to stage UFO sightings.

How big is the Universe?

The observable Universe (the part that can be seen from Earth) is thought to be 93 billion light-years across – that's how far light has travelled in its 13.8-billion-year lifetime. But the Universe's expansion means that some objects are further away than that – their light just hasn't had enough time to reach us yet. Because we can't see beyond that, we can't know the true size of the entire Universe.

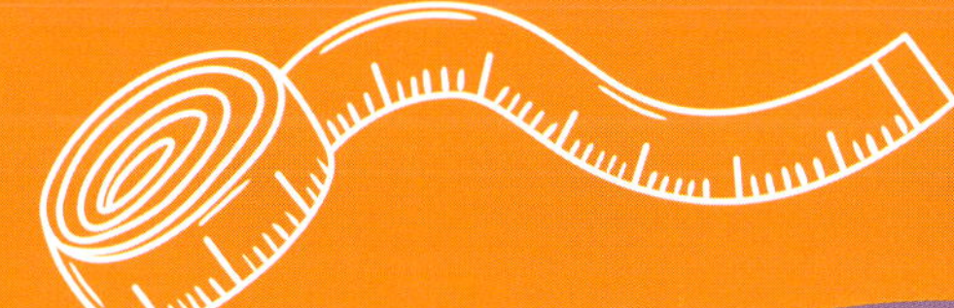

Could there be a multiverse?

For centuries, people have been fascinated by the idea of other worlds – and now that we understand more about the far reaches of our expanding Universe, we're also intrigued by what lies beyond. One idea is that there could be many other universes – called the 'multiverse'. For now, this is just science fiction, but who knows what we might discover in the future?

Glossary

aphelion: the point in a planet or comet's orbit when it is furthest from the Sun.

asterism: a well-known, unofficial pattern of stars.

asteroid: a small, rocky object that orbits the Sun.

astrology: the study of the movements of the planets, Sun, Moon, and stars in the belief that these movements can affect people's lives.

atmosphere: the layer of air or other gases around a planet.

atom: the basic building block for all matter in the Universe.

aurora: dazzling displays of colourful light that move across the sky, mainly in the polar regions of a planet.

Big Bang: a widely believed theory that suggests that the Universe was created as a result of a huge explosion.

black hole: an object in space where gravity is so strong that nothing, not even light, can escape.

charged particles: a particle with a positive or negative charge, such as an electron, proton, or helium ion.

coma: a cloud of gas and dust surrounding the nucleus of a comet.

comet: an icy, rocky object that travels around the Sun and can sometimes have a tail of gas and dust.

constellation: an officially named pattern of stars.

core: the central part of a planet.

corona: the Sun's outer atmosphere.

coronal mass ejection (CME): a cloud of particles ejected from the Sun's surface during a solar flare.

crater: a bowl-shaped hole on the surface of an object, which has been caused by something impacting it.

crust: the Earth's outer layer.

dark energy: invisible 'energy' that is believed to make the Universe expand faster and faster.

dark matter: material that is believed to form a large part of the Universe, but has never been seen.

dwarf planet: an object in space that is similar to a planet, but smaller. Dwarf planets do not have a clear path around the Sun.

eccentric: used to describe how round or oval-shaped an orbit is.

electron: a negatively charged particle found in an atom, spinning around the outside of the nucleus.

elliptical: having an oval shape.

equator: an imaginary line around the middle of the Earth.

equinox: one of the two days in the year when the hours of day and night are of equal length.

exoplanet: a planet that orbits a star other than our Sun.

infrared: a type of light that humans can't see.

interplanetary: between different planets.

interstellar: between different stars.

ion: an electrically charged atom.

joule: a unit of energy.

Kuiper Belt: a doughnut-shaped region of icy objects beyond Neptune's orbit.

light pollution: the glow from streetlights and buildings that brightens the night sky and makes it difficult to see the stars.

light-year: the distance that light travels in a year.

lunar eclipse: when the Earth moves in front of the Sun and blocks its light from reaching the Moon.

mantle layer: the part of the Earth between the crust and the core.

maria: dark patches on the Moon. 'Maria' is the word for multiple patches; 'mare' is just one.

meteor: a small object from outer space that burns very brightly when it enters the Earth's atmosphere.

meteorite: a piece of rock or metal from space that has landed on Earth.

meteoroid: small lumps of rock or metal travelling through outer space.

Milky Way: our galaxy.

molten: heated to a very high temperature to become a hot, thick liquid.

nebula: a cloud of dust and gas in space.

neutron: an atomic particle that has no electrical charge.

Northern Hemisphere: the half of the Earth that is north of the equator.

nucleus: the central part of an object like an atom or a comet.

Oort cloud: a spherical cloud of icy objects including comets orbiting the Sun, far beyond Pluto and the Kuiper Belt.

particle: a piece of matter smaller than an atom, like an electron or a proton.

perihelion: the point in a planet or comet's orbit when it is closest to the Sun.

phases of the Moon: the differing appearances of the Moon as we see it from Earth.

prism: a block of clear glass or plastic which separates the light passing through it into different colours, like a rainbow.

probe: a robotic spacecraft that travels into space, with no people in it, to study objects in the Solar System and beyond, and send information back to Earth.

proton: a positively charged particle found in the centre of an atom, inside the nucleus.

radiation: energy that travels from one place to another, like light or heat. Sometimes it can be dangerous to us.

solar eclipse: the total or partial covering of the Sun by the Moon.

solar filter: a lens added to a telescope to protect the eyes from the Sun's bright light.

solar flare: a sudden, bright burst of energy on the Sun's surface.

solar panel: a panel that takes in sunlight and turns it into electricity.

solar prominence: a big cloud of plasma that erupts from the Sun's surface.

solar storm: a sudden explosion of particles, energy, magnetic fields, and material from the Sun, which affects the Earth.

Solar System: the Sun and everything that orbits around it, including planets, moons, dwarf planets, comets and asteroids.

solar wind: a flow of charged particles from the Sun that travel out in all directions.

solstice: the two points in the year when a planet's axis is most-tilted towards or away from the Sun, giving us the longest and shortest days of the year measured by hours of daylight.

Southern Hemisphere: the half of the Earth that is south of the equator.

stellar: used to describe anything related to stars.

sunspot: a dark, cooler patch on the Sun's surface.

supernova: an exploding star.

tectonic: relating to the structure of the Earth's surface or crust.

thruster: a small rocket engine on a spacecraft.

transit method: the process of watching a star's light dim as a planet passes in front of it.

weathering: the breaking down of rocks as a result of being exposed to the elements, like rain or wind.

zodiac constellation: the constellations after which the signs of the zodiac are named: Aries, Taurus, Gemini, Cancer, Leo, Virgo, Libra, Scorpio, Sagittarius, Capricorn, Aquarius, and Pisces.

Index

A
accretion disk 124
achondrites 75
active galactic nucleus 110–11
Aditya-L1 87, 103
albedo effect 63
Andromeda 106, 114, 116
Apollo missions 52, 55
Arecibo 137
Armstrong, Neil 52
Artemis mission 53
asterisms 91, 99
Asteroid Belt 6, 70
asteroid-moons 56
asteroids 32, 41, 56–7, 62, 66–7, 71, 74–5, 79–81
  Trojan 31, 66
astrology 24, 101
astronauts 52–3, 55
atmospheres
  gas planets 30–1, 34, 37–9, 45
  moons 52, 58–9, 61–2
  rocky planets 12–16, 21, 23
  space rocks 66, 76
atoms 84, 122–3
auroras 23, 38, 96, 100
axis 9, 13, 15, 22

B
Bennu 67, 81
Betelgeuse 92, 97
Big Bang 122–3, 129, 138
Big Bounce 131
Big Chill/Freeze 131
Big Crunch 131
Big Rip 131
black holes 97, 124–7, 131, 133, 135
  supermassive 91, 107, 110, 114, 125
blazars 110
blue giants 89
brown dwarfs 88

C
Carrington Event 100
Cassini-Huygens probe 31, 33, 45
Centaurus A 111
Ceres 57, 70
Charon 57, 61
Chicagohenge 22
Chicxulub Crater 79
chondrites 75
circumpolar stars 98
comets 32, 41, 66, 68–9, 74–7, 79–80
constellations 76, 98–101
coronal mass ejections 87, 97, 100
Crab Nebula 97
craters 12, 20–1, 49, 55, 57, 62, 74, 79

D
Dactyl 56
dark energy 123, 129–30, 134, 138
dark matter 115, 128–30, 134, 138
DART mission 81
day 86
Daylight Saving Time 23
Deimos 18, 62
density 9, 13, 32, 122
diamond 37, 75
Dimorphos 81
dinosaurs, extinction 79
dwarf planets 36, 56–7, 61, 70–1, 75, 77, 80, 96

E
Earth 7–9, 13–18, 20–7, 40–1, 48–51, 58, 74, 90, 96, 99–100
  age 87
Earthrise photo 55
Earthshine 51
eclipses 50, 94–5
Einstein, Albert 127, 133
Enceladus 58, 63
Encke 79
equinoxes 22
Eris 70–1
ESA 7, 26, 80, 102–3, 134
Euclid mission 134–5
Europa 30, 43, 58, 60
event horizon 124
exoplanets 72–3, 75, 78, 81, 136–7
Extremely Large Telescope 136
extremophiles 17

F
flybys 7, 13–15, 18, 30–1, 33, 35–7
forces 8

G
Gaia mission 118–19
galaxies 4, 104–19, 123, 125, 128
  active 110–11
  collision 114
  dwarf 106–7, 109
  elliptical 108–9
  interacting 109
  irregular 108
  lenticular 108
  radio 110–11
  ring 109
  Seyfert 110
  spiral 107, 108–9
  starburst 109
  ultra-diffuse (dark) 109
  zombie 115
  see also specific galaxies
Galileo Galilei 24, 43
gases 9, 39, 68, 86
geocentric model 24–5
Goldilocks Zone 16, 72
gravitational waves 126–7, 135
gravity 8, 13, 21, 27, 62, 123, 128–9, 133
  and asteroids 67
  and black holes 124
  and gas planets 30, 32, 34, 36, 41, 80
  and mini moons 57
  and space rocks 67, 74, 75
  and stars 85, 112–14
gravity assists 27
Great Bombardment 78

H
Hafele-Keating experiment 133
Halley's Comet 69
Haumea 70
heliocentric model 25, 100
helium 86, 90, 123
Herschel, William 35, 42
Higgs boson 130
Hubble, Edwin 115, 116
Hubble Space Telescope 36, 44, 116, 118–19, 134
Huygens probe 60
hydrogen 86, 90, 123

I
Ida (asteroid) 56
impactors 7, 81
Io 30, 43, 56, 61, 63
iron 13, 16, 19–21, 48, 67, 79

J
James Webb Space Telescope 44–5, 115, 118, 134
Jodrell Bank 136–7
JUNO probe 45
Jupiter 7, 24, 30–2, 37–9, 41–3, 45, 80
  Great Red Spot 31, 41
  moons 30–1, 41, 43, 45, 56, 58, 60–1, 63
JUpiter ICy moon Explorer 31, 45

K
Kepler telescope 73, 81, 136–7
Kepler-90 72–3, 136
Kuiper Belt 5, 6, 36, 69

L
landers 7, 14–15, 18–19, 80
Large Hadron Collider 130, 135
Large Magellanic Cloud 107–8
life 14, 16–17, 25, 27, 58–9, 72, 78, 86, 136–7, 139
light 8, 19, 39, 84, 90, 97, 124
  speed of 8, 122, 127, 135
light-years 85, 99
LIGO 126–7, 135
liquids 9, 39, 68
LISA 135
Local Group 106

M
magnetic fields 8, 16, 20–1, 23, 30, 32, 38–9, 87, 96
Makemake 70
Mars 6, 7, 15–16, 18–21, 24–7, 42, 62–3
mass 8
matter 9
Mercury 7, 12–13, 20–2, 24, 26–7, 90, 129

Messier objects 117
meteorites 66–7, 75, 79, 137
meteors 66–7, 76
Milky Way 4, 72, 88, 101, 106–7, 112–14, 116, 118
Mimas 57
moon dogs 51
Moon (Earth's) 40, 48–55, 59, 62, 75, 94–5
moons 18, 30–1, 34–6, 41, 43, 45–63
  mini 57
motion 9
multiplanetary systems 72
multiverse 139

N
NASA 7, 27, 45, 55, 60, 81, 101, 103, 136–7
nebulae 91, 97
  fuzzy 116–17
Neptune 6, 7, 36–7, 39, 41–3, 45, 61, 77, 129
neutrinos 122, 132
neutron stars 91, 126
New Horizons 44, 61, 80
night 86
North Star 98–9
nuclear fusion 84, 85

O
occultation 40
Oort Cloud 5, 69
opposition 40
orbiters 7, 13–15, 18–19, 31, 33, 86–7, 118–19, 134–5, 137
orbits 9, 40, 50, 100
  dwarf planets 70, 77
  eccentric 12, 69
  egg-shaped 23
  elliptical 48
  galactic 106

P
P/Shoemaker-Levy 9 comet 41
pallasites 67
pareidolia 21
Parker Solar Probe 87, 102
particles 122–3, 132–3, 135
perihelion 23, 77
Phobos 18, 62, 63
phosphine 14
Pillars of Creation 134
planets 6–7, 75
  gas 7, 28–45, 72
  minor 71
  rocky 7, 10–27, 41, 72
  shape 21
  see also specific planets
plasma 9, 84, 93, 97
plate tectonics 17, 74
Pleiades 112
Plough 99
Pluto 57, 61, 70–1, 75, 77, 80, 96
polar ice 20
pressure 14, 27, 37
Proxima Centauri b 73

Q
quantum mechanics 133
quasars 110, 137
quasi-moons 57
quenching 114

R
red dwarfs 88
red giants 89, 90
Red Monsters 115
redshift 115
relativity 127, 133
rings 32, 37–8, 45
rotation 9, 15
rovers 7, 19, 27

S
sample return 7, 19, 80–1
satellites 16–17, 27
Saturn 6–7, 24, 27, 30, 32–3, 38–9, 41–3, 45, 57–63
SDO 87, 103
seasons 13, 22, 99
SETI 137
shooting stars 66
singularities 138
Sloan Digital Sky Survey 119
Small Magellanic Cloud 107–8
SOHO orbiter 86, 103
solar eclipses 94–5
solar flares 87, 97
solar max/min 96
Solar Orbiter 87, 102
solar prominence 87, 93
Solar Systems 5–7, 24–5, 41–2, 66, 68–72, 74, 90, 106
solar wind 13, 23, 38, 96
solids 9, 39
solstices 22
space agencies 7
  see also ESA; NASA
space missions 13–19, 26–7, 30–1, 33–7, 44–5, 52–3, 55–6, 60–1, 80–1, 86–7, 102–3, 118–19, 134–7
space rocks 64–81
space-time 127
spaghettification 124
star clusters 112–13
stardust 90
stars 5, 82–103, 106–7, 109, 114–15, 123, 126, 129–30, 134
  colours 85, 93
  definition 44–5
  guest 97
  lifecycle 85, 87, 90–1
  temperature 85, 93
  types 88–9
  variable 92, 116
  see also specific stars
storms 30–3, 36, 38
sublimation 68
Sun 6–7, 9, 86–7, 101, 106
  age 87
  corona 87, 93, 95, 96
  energy 84, 86
  fuel 86, 90
  and gas planets 36, 40–1
  gravity 12, 27
  heliocentric model 25, 100
  and lunar eclipses 50
  magnetic field 87, 96
  and rocky planets 7, 12–13, 16, 22–3, 26, 50
  siblings 112
  and solar eclipses 94–5
  solar missions 86–7, 102–3
  and space rocks 67–71, 76–7
  temperature 93
  as yellow dwarf 88
sunsets 19
sunspots 87, 96
super-Earths 72–3
supermoons 51
supernovas 91–2, 97, 126

T
tektites 67
temperature 12, 14, 27, 34–5, 37
TESS 137
tidal locking 49
time dilation 125, 133
Titan 43, 45, 59, 60–1, 63
trans-Neptunian objects 71
transit method 73
Triangulum 106
Triton 36, 61
Tycho crater 49, 62

U
UFOs 139
Universe 4–5, 99, 119, 130–5, 138–9
  expansion 115, 122–3, 129, 131, 133, 138–9
  size 139
  static 133
Uranus 7, 34–5, 39, 41–4, 61
Usagi 54

V
Valles Marineris 19
Venus 6–7, 14–16, 20–4, 27, 40, 90
Very Large Telescope 136
volcanoes 14, 16–21, 34, 61, 63
Voyager 30, 33, 35–6, 44–5, 61

W
water 15–16, 20, 32, 58–9, 63
weight 8
white dwarfs 89, 91, 97
wormholes 132

Y
yellow dwarfs 88

Z
zodiac 101

Images

Whilst every effort has been made to trace the copyright owners of the images used in this book, in cases where this has been unsuccessful, or if any have inadvertently been overlooked, the publishers would gladly receive any information enabling them to rectify any error or omission at the first opportunity.

p2 (+p6 p19 p20 p26), Mars: NASA/JPL/USGS. **p3 (+p27)**, Venus: NASA/JPL-Caltech. **pp4-5 (+p138)**, background: NASA, ESA, G. Illingworth, D. Magee, and P. Oesch (University of California, Santa Cruz), R. Bouwens (Leiden University), and the HUDF09 Team. **p5 (+p69)**, Solar System: ESA (acknowledgement: work performed by ATG under contract to ESA); CC BY-SA 3.0 IGO. **p7 (+p119)**, Hubble: NASA. **p12**, Magritte: NASA/Johns Hopkins University Applied Physics Laboratory/Carnegie Institution of Washington. **p14**, volcano: ESA/AOES. **p15**, BepiColombo: NASA. **p18**, Olympus Mons: NASA/JPL/USGS. **p19**, sunset: NASA/JPL/Texas A&M/Cornell. **p21**, Galle: NASA/JPL-Caltech/MSSS. **p24**, phases: Science History Images/Alamy Stock Photo. **p25**, geocentric: The Print Collector/Alamy Stock Photo. **p26**, Ingenuity: NASA/JPL-Caltech. **p30**, moons: NASA/JPL-Caltech/SwRI/MSSS/Kevin M. Gill. **p32**, rings: Science Photo Library/Alamy Stock Photo. **p33**, vortex: NASA/JPL-Caltech/Space Science Institute. **p34**, Miranda: NASA/JPL-Caltech. **p34**, Earth & Uranus: NASA. **p35**, W. Herschel: Pictorial Press Ltd/Alamy Stock Photo. **p38**, cyclones: NASA/JPL-Caltech/SwRI/ASI/INAF/JIRAM. **p38**, auroras: NASA, ESA, and J. Nichols (University of Leicester); Acknowledgment: A. Simon (NASA/GSFC) and the OPAL team. **p39**, diagram: NASA/Lunar and Planetary Institute (fonts changed). **p41**, P/Shoemaker-Levy 9: Everett Collection Historical/Alamy Stock Photo. **p41**, shadows: NASA, ESA, and the Hubble Heritage Team (STScI/AURA). **p43**, moons: NASA/JPL/DLR. **p45**, Neptune: NASA, ESA, CSA, STScI. **p52**, B. Aldrin: Archive Image/Alamy Stock Photo. **p53**, near side: NASA/Goddard Space Flight Center/Arizona State University. **p53**, boot print: NASA/Buzz Aldrin. **p55**, control centre: NC Collections/Alamy Stock Photo. **p55**, Earthrise: NASA. **p56**, Ida & Dactyl: NASA/JPL. **p56**, Io: NASA/JPL/University of Arizona. **p57**, Mimas: NASA/JPL-Caltech/Space Science Institute. **p57**, Death Star: LANDMARK MEDIA/Alamy Stock Photo. **p58**, Europa: NASA/JPL-Caltech/SwRI/MSSS/Kevin M. Gill. **p58**, Enceladus: NASA/JPL-Caltech/Space Science Institute. **p59**, polar region: NASA/JPL-Caltech/ASI/USGS. **p59**, visible light: NASA/JPL-Caltech/SSI/Kevin M. Gill. **p59**, infrared light: Science History Images/Alamy Stock Photo. **p59**, mare: NASA/GSFC/Arizona State University. **p60**, Titan surface: World History Archive/Alamy Stock Photo. **p61**, Charon: J Marshall – Tribaleye Images/Alamy Stock Photo. **p61**, Triton: NASA/JPL. **p61**, Voyager: NASA/JPL. **p62**, crater: NASA. **p62**, Pan: NASA/JPL-Caltech/Space Science Institute. **p63**, stripes: World History Archive/Alamy Stock Photo. **p63**, eruption: Science Photo Library/Alamy Stock Photo. **p66**, Vesta: NASA/JPL/MPS/DLR/IDA/Björn Jónsson. **p67**, 433 Eros: NASA/JPL/JHUAPL. **p67**, 101955 Bennu: NASA/Goddard/University of Arizona. **p69**, Halley's comet: NASA/W. Liller. **p72**, Kepler exoplanets: NASA/Ames Research Center/Wendy Stenzel. **p73**, Proxima Centauri b: Science History Images/Alamy Stock Photo. **p75**, Comet 67P: ESA/Rosetta/NAVCAM; CC BY-SA IGO 3.0. **p77**, meteor shower: Alan Dyer/VWPics/Alamy Stock Photo. **p78**, Bayeux Tapestry: GRANGER – Historical Picture Archive/Alamy Stock Photo. **p79**, Chicxulub Crater: Science Photo Library/Alamy Stock Photo. **p79**, Campo del Cielo: National Space Centre. **p79**, Encke: Jim Scotti. **p80**, New Horizons: NASA. **p81**, Kepler: NASA/JPL-Caltech. **p81**, DART: Science Photo Library/Alamy Stock Photo. **p85**, forces in the Sun: TIM BROWN/SCIENCE PHOTO LIBRARY. **p87**, sunspots: NASA/SDO. **p88**, AU Mic: NASA's Goddard Space Flight Center/Chris Smith (USRA). **p88**, 2MASSJ22282889-431026: ADC PICTURES/Alamy Stock Photo. **p89**, AG Carinae: NASA, ESA, STScI. **p89**, white dwarf: NG Images/Alamy Stock Photo. **p93**, stars: NASA, ESA, Thomas Brown. **p94**, total eclipse: NASA/Keegan Barber. **p94**, partial eclipse: David Trudgian. **p95**, eclipse shadow: NASA. **p95**, pinhole projector: National Space Centre. **p97**, solar explosion: American Photo Archive/Alamy Stock Photo. **p101**, N.G. Roman: NASA. **p102**, Parker Solar Probe: NASA. **p102**, Solar Orbiter: ESA/ATG medialab. **p103**, SOHO: Alex Lutkus. **p103**, SDO: NASA. **p107**, Milky Way: Stocktrek Images, Inc./Alamy Stock Photo. **p107**, spiral galaxy: Universal Images Group North America LLC/Alamy Stock Photo. **p108**, NGC 1300: NASA, ESA, and the Hubble Heritage Team (STScI/AURA). **p108**, Abell S0740: NASA, ESA, and the Hubble Heritage Team (STScI/AURA). **p108**, NGC 2337: ESA/Hubble & NASA. **p108**, NGC 4866: ESA/Hubble & NASA; Acknowledgment: Gilles Chapdelaine. **p109**, NGC 5264: ESA/Hubble & NASA. **p109**, M82: NASA, ESA and the Hubble Heritage Team (STScI/AURA). Acknowledgment: J. Gallagher (University of Wisconsin), M. Mountain (STScI) and P. Puxley (NSF). **p109**, Arp 142: NASA-ESA/STScI/AURA/JPL-Caltech. **p109**, Hoag's Object: NASA and the Hubble Heritage Team (STScI/AURA); Acknowledgment: Ray A. Lucas (STScI/AURA). **p109**, NGC 1052-DF2: NASA, ESA, and P. van Dokkum (Yale University). **p110**, NGC 5728: ESA/Hubble, A. Riess et al., J. Greene; CC BY 4.0. **p110**, NGC 5128: Science Photo Library/Alamy Stock Photo. **p110**, blazar: NASA/JPL-Caltech/GSFC. **p111**, Centaurus A: ESO/WFI (Optical); MPIfR/ESO/APEX/A.Weiss et al. (Submillimetre); NASA/CXC/CfA/R.Kraft et al. (X-ray); CC 4.0. **p111**, Hercules A: NASA, ESA, S. Baum and C. O'Dea (RIT), R. Perley and W. Cotton (NRAO/AUI/NSF), and the Hubble Heritage Team (STScI/AURA). **p112**, Pleiades: NASA, ESA and AURA/Caltech. **p113**, Coma: Alberto Pisabarro; CC 4.0. **p114**, Arp 143: NASA, ESA, STScI, and J. Dalcanton (Center for Computational Astrophysics/Flatiron Inst., UWashington). **p115**, red monsters: NASA/CSA/ESA, M. Xiao & P. A. Oesch (University of Geneva), G. Brammer (Niels Bohr Institute), Dawn JWST Archive. **p115**, MACS2129-1: NASA, ESA, and Z. Levy (STScI). **p116**, Hubble Deep Field: Robert Williams (NASA, ESA, STScI). **p117**, C. Messier: GL Archive/Alamy Stock Photo. **p118**, Gaia: Science History Images/Alamy Stock Photo. **p118**, JWST: NASA. **p118**, JWST in rocket: ESA/D. Ducros. **p119**, Hubble launch: NASA. **pp122-3**, diagram: NASA (fonts changed). **p125**, M87: Event Horizon Telescope Collaboration. **p127**, Einstein: Alpha Historica/Alamy Stock Photo. **p128**, Coma Cluster: NASA, ESA/Hubble, HST Frontier Fields. **p129**, V. Rubin: Carnegie Institution for Science; CC 4.0. **p131**, expanding universe: MARK GARLICK/SCIENCE PHOTO LIBRARY. **p133**, Cygnus X-1: NASA/CXC/SAO. **p133**, Einstein: GL Archive/Alamy Stock Photo. **p135**, LISA: ESA. **p136**, Kepler: NASA. **p137**, TESS: NASA-GSFC. **p137**, Arecibo message: fabrizio annovi/Alamy Stock Vector. All other images & illustrations © Shutterstock.